The R
King o...

Sheila K. McCullagh

Nelson

When Nicholas's great-uncle Jeremy was lost at sea, he left Nicholas a picture. It was a picture of a great ring of silver, against a black background. There was a picture inside the silver ring, too. Most of the time, it was just the sea and the sky. But sometimes the picture changed and Nicholas found himself looking right through the ring, into another country.

In some strange way, when the ring glowed like silver fire it grew very large, and Nicholas found himself moving right through it, into the country in the centre of the ring.

Sometimes, he found himself on a ship; sometimes on dry land. But wherever he was, he found himself among the buccaneers of Ramir, who had become his friends.

This is another of Nicholas's adventures.

Chapter 1
Traitors in Ramir

Nicholas was coming home from school. As he turned into his own street, he saw three boys standing near some railings. He knew two of them. They were in his class at school. Their names were Jack and Fred, and Nicholas didn't like them. The third boy was about a year younger. Nicholas hadn't seen him before.

As Nicholas turned the corner, Jack slapped the younger boy across the face.

"What do you think you're doing?" said Nicholas, as he came up to them.

Jack turned towards him.

"He's a new boy," he said. "I'm just teaching him manners."

"You'd better learn some yourself," said Nicholas. "Shove off!"

"I don't mind giving you a lesson, too," said Jack, clenching his fist.

"Look out!" said Fred. "Someone's coming."

A man had come out of a house down the road, next door to the one where Nicholas lived. He was walking quickly towards them.

"I'll see you later," said Jack.

He ran off around the corner, and out of the street, with Fred at his heels.

"What's happening, Alan?" asked the man, as he came up to them.

"Nothing. It's all right, Dad. Just a bit of

an argument," said the boy. He jerked his head towards Nicholas. "He was helping me," he said.

"So I saw," said the man. "What's your name?"

Nicholas stared at him. He was so surprised, that he couldn't answer straight away. The man looked so like Captain Francis Harken of the buccaneers in Ramir, that for a moment Nicholas thought Captain Harken must have come through the silver ring. But then he saw that this man was different.

He pulled himself together.

"I'm Nicholas Strange," he said.

"I saw you go off to school this morning," said the boy. "We've just moved into the house next door to you."

"I didn't know," said Nicholas.

"Well, I'm glad we've got a friend next door," said the man. "My name's Tregarth — Andrew Tregarth. And this is my son, Alan. You must come in and see us.

"I've got to go down to the town now, Alan, and you'll have to come with me. We've got to see Mr. Tell again. But I hope we'll see you later, Nicholas."

He nodded to Nicholas, and went on down the road.

"See you!" said Alan, grinning cheerfully. He ran off, after his father.

Nicholas walked slowly along to his own house. He still felt shaken by the meeting. The man had looked so like Captain Harken.

And when he came to think about it, Alan was rather like Alanni, the boy he had met when he was looking for treasure in Ramir.

As he turned in at the gate, he saw that the 'For Sale' sign had gone from the house next door. There were curtains in the windows.

"Is that you, Nicholas?" called his mother, as he opened the front door.

"Yes," said Nicholas, going into the kitchen. "The house next door has been sold."

"The new people moved in yesterday," said his mother. "Hadn't you noticed?"

Nicholas shook his head.

"You live too much in a world of your own," said his mother. "There's a boy next door now. He might be a friend for you."

"I just met him," said Nicholas. "His name's Alan."

"Well, I'm glad," said his mother.

At that point, Nicholas's step-father came in, and they started talking of other things. But when he went to bed, Nicholas was still thinking about Andrew Tregarth, and Alan, and Captain Harken.

* * *

He had been asleep for only a short time, when he woke with a start. He threw back the bedclothes, got out of bed, and went over to the window. A full moon was shining down on the roofs of the houses and the streets of the city. Most of the windows in the houses opposite were dark.

Far away, he heard a clock striking. He counted the strokes. Twelve. It was midnight.

He stared out over the city. The moonlight was very bright. It had been raining earlier in the night, and the wet roofs shone like silver.

As he looked, the moonlight seemed to grow even brighter. It seemed to be all around him, as if a silver waterfall was pouring into the room.

A feeling of excitement shot up inside him, like water in a fountain when the tap is turned on. He turned quickly to look at the picture on the wall. When he had got into bed, the picture had shown only a dull ring of silver, with waves of the sea in the middle of it. But now the ring was shining as brightly as the moon.

Nicholas ran across the room, and stared into the ring. The picture had changed. He could see a dark space, with stone walls. It was a narrow passage. Light was coming into the passage through holes in a stone carving in the far wall.

Nicholas drew in his breath quickly. It looked like the hidden room in the wall of the Council Chamber of Ramir, and yet it wasn't quite the same. The carving was stone, not wood. It was smaller, and the passage was narrower.

Nicholas took a step towards the picture. The silver light flared up into flames, which grew so bright that he shut his eyes.

When he opened them again, the flames had died away. He found himself standing in the dark passage, dressed in the white shirt and blue trousers that he always wore in the Country of Ramir.

The passage disappeared into the darkness on each side of him, but there was a light in the room on the far side of the stone wall.

Nicholas moved closer to the stone carving, and looked through the holes, into the room beyond.

It was a big, square room. There seemed to be windows on three sides, but wooden shutters had been pulled across the windows. A fire was burning in the hearth, in the middle of the wall opposite him. There was a bed against another wall, and a chair and table stood in the middle of the room.

The room was lit by two lanterns, which hung from brackets in the wall on each side of the fire. There was no one there.

As Nicholas gazed in through the holes in the stone carving, a door opened on his left, in the same wall.

Two boys came into the room, followed by a man. The man was wearing a grey cloak, trimmed with white fur. Nicholas drew in his breath sharply. He recognised all three of them. The first boy, a year or two older than he was, was the Alarkin, the son of the old Lord of Ramir. The second boy, who was almost a man, was the Alarkool, the Alarkin's older brother. And the man in the grey cloak was Soluken, the Regent of Ramir.

The Alarkin stumbled forwards, as if he had been pushed. Nicholas saw that his hands were tied behind his back.

The Alarkool caught the boy's shoulder, and stopped him from falling. Soluken shut the door behind them.

The Alarkool pulled out a knife, and cut the ropes tying his brother's hands.

"There," he said. "You're free now. Sit down on the bed."

"Free?" asked the Alarkin, turning to face the Alarkool. "Free to leave this tower?"

"Don't be a fool, Alarkin," said Soluken. "You know very well what we mean. You will not leave this tower until your brother is crowned King of Ramir. And until you have sworn to obey him."

"I am the rightful King of Ramir," said the Alarkin. "My father said so. I was chosen by the Council, when I brought the Crown of Ramir back from the land of the Nebohni."

"The Council of Ramir had no right to choose you," said the Alarkool fiercely. "You know that. I am older than you are. The Council has always chosen the Lord of Ramir's eldest son to be ruler after him."

"They have the right to choose whoever they wish," said the Alarkin. "So had my father. And my father chose me. He said that I was to be Lord of Ramir after him. The Council agreed with him."

"We have a new Council now, Alarkin," said Soluken. "You know that. And your father is dead." Nicholas could hear the anger in his voice. "The new Council has made another choice — a better choice."

"They're not the true Council of Ramir!" cried the Alarkin, tossing back his head. "They were not chosen by the people. They are your friends — or should I say, your puppets?"

Soluken stepped forward and lifted his hand. He would have struck the Alarkin across the face, but the Alarkool caught his arm.

"Soluken! The Alarkin may be a prisoner, but he is still my brother," he said coldly. "You will not strike him.

"There is no point in talking about this any more, Alarkin. You will stay here, in this tower, until you promise to obey me.

"Gunrun will be your servant and also your guard. You have no chance of escape. You will remain here, until I have been crowned King of Ramir, and until everyone in Ramir accepts me as their ruler.

"No one will harm you — unless you do anything foolish. But I don't think there is anything you can do. You will be given books, but you won't be allowed to write, or to send any messages to your friends. Gunrun will not help you. He has always been my faithful servant, and he will do exactly as I say.

"You can have anything you want, to make you more comfortable. But you will stay here, until I decide to set you free."

"I shall grow old here, if I wait till then!" said the Alarkin.

"Perhaps you will," said the Alarkool. "But that depends on you. Swear to obey me, and I will let you go, once I am king."

"My friends will never let you become king, Alarkool," said the Alarkin. "Do you think the buccaneers will sit by, and do nothing, while you take over the kingdom of Ramir?"

"Don't think you'll get any help from the buccaneers," said the Alarkool coldly. "If you're expecting them to help you, you'll wait a long time. *The Silver Dolphin* and *The Blue Whale* are anchored in the Sea Road. The Council has sent orders to Captain Harken to sail in the morning. He is to go back to Ikroon, with Martin Quinn, to try and recover the Sea-king's treasure from the bottom of the sea."

"But that's an impossible task!" cried the Alarkin. "You heard Martin Quinn say that it went down in the deep channel. They'll never be able to recover it now."

"I care very little whether they bring back the treasure or not," said the Alarkool. "But their orders are to sail in the morning. They will leave the Sea Road of Ramir at first light, and I doubt very much whether they will be back in less than a year.

"The rest of the fleet sailed south three days ago, and will not return until the spring. By that time I shall be crowned King of Ramir, and the city will be in our hands."

"The city is already ours," said Soluken. "My own men took over guard duty tonight. In a week's time, the new Council will proclaim the Alarkool king. And I have more than enough men in the city who are in my pay, to make sure that no one makes any trouble. If they do, there is plenty of room for them in the prisons of Ramir."

"You have nothing to lose by promising to obey me," said the Alarkool. "As you see, the city is mine already."

The Alarkin said nothing, but Nicholas could see from the expression on his face that he was not going to promise anything.

The Alarkool went to the door, and opened it.

"Gunrun!" he called.

"Here, Alarkool of Ramir!" Nicholas heard a deep voice answer.

A big man came through the doorway into the room. He was much taller and broader than any of the others, and he had rough, dark hair, which fell forward over his forehead.

"Gunrun, you will look after the Alarkin," said the Alarkool. "You will bring him food and drink, and wood for the fire. You will keep this room clean for him, and you will

13

treat him with respect. Remember that he is my brother.

"But you are also his guard. I shall hold you responsible for his safety. Bring him anything he wants, that will make him more comfortable. But bring him nothing that may help him to escape. And do not take any messages to anyone, except me. Do you understand?"

"I understand, Alarkool of Ramir," said Gunrun. "I'll guard him."

The Alarkool nodded, and turned to the Alarkin.

"I will leave you now," he said. "Gunrun will bring your supper. Remember what I have said. You will be safe here, as long as you don't try to do anything foolish."

The Alarkin said nothing.

The Alarkool looked at him for a few moments. Then he turned, and went out of the room, followed by Soluken.

The Alarkin sat down on the bed. Gunrun looked across at him, but he still said nothing, and after a minute or two, Gunrun left the room. Nicholas heard him shoot the bolts on the other side of the door.

Nicholas was still wondering what to do, when he heard the bolts being drawn back again. The door opened, and Gunrun came in with a tray. There was a plate of food on it, and a drinking horn.

Gunrun didn't speak. He put the tray

down on the table, and went out again, bolting the door behind him.

Nicholas put his mouth to the holes in the stone carving.

"Alarkin!" he whispered. "Alarkin!"

The Alarkin looked up, listening.

"Alarkin!" whispered Nicholas again.

"Who's speaking?" said the Alarkin sharply.

"Sh!" whispered Nicholas. "It's me, Nicholas Strange. I'm in a passage in the wall, behind the stone carving."

"How on earth did you get there, Nicholas?" cried the Alarkin.

"Sh!" whispered Nicholas again. "I don't know who's about, or if anyone can hear me. And I don't really know where I am. I've just come through the silver ring. I came through from The Other Side, and found myself here. I saw the Alarkool and Soluken bring you here, and I heard what they said. Where are we?"

"You're in the old tower, that stands in the wall around the City of Ramir," said the Alarkin, coming over to the stone carving, and speaking softly. "One side of the tower faces out, into the mountains. The other looks across the city, to the Sea Road of Ramir.

"Are you really in a secret passage? Or is it just a hole in the wall?"

"I think it's a passage," said Nicholas.

"I'll have to find out. I'm going to try and find my way to the Sea Road, and *The Silver Dolphin,* before Captain Harken sails. But I wanted to tell you first."

"I can scarcely believe that you're there, Nick — except that you do always seem to turn up, just when you're needed.

"You'll have to be quick, to get to Captain Harken before he sails. And did you hear what Soluken said? The guards have been changed. They're all his men."

"I heard that," said Nicholas. "I'll do the best I can. I'll have to go now. But I just wanted to tell you, before I left."

"Go as quickly as you can, Nick," said the Alarkin. "Don't get caught! And good luck go with you."

Nicholas looked quickly up and down the passage. His eyes were more used to the dim light now. There were steps leading down to his left. To his right, the passage ended a few metres away, in what looked like a door.

He went over to the door, and felt it with his hands. He touched a metal ring. He twisted the ring sideways, and heard a latch click up. The door opened into darkness.

Nicholas felt carefully with his hands, and found that he was at the foot of some more steps. He begain to climb them very slowly, feeling his way.

He was going up a narrow spiral staircase.

His head bumped against the roof. He lifted his hands, and felt a big flat stone above him. When he pushed on it, it lifted at one side.

Nicholas pushed hard. The stone swung upwards and his head came out into the fresh air. He pushed the stone fully back, and climbed carefully out.

He found himself standing in the top of a turret on a high tower. The moon was shining down, and he could see quite clearly.

There was a turret on each corner of the tower. There were stone battlements all around the top, and smaller ones around each turret.

Nicholas looked out between the battlements, and saw the City of Ramir lying below him.

The tower had been built at the highest point of the city wall, on the mountain side behind Ramir. Nicholas saw the wall stretching away to the left and right, and then climbing down the mountains to the Sea Road of Ramir — the narrow channel of water that led between the mountains out to the open sea. He could see a long way up the Sea Road. He could even see a great rock, sticking out into the channel below the mountains to his left.

Nicholas's eyes came back to the tower.

There was a door in the turret opposite him, but as he looked across at it, he heard bolts being drawn back.

Nicholas dropped down behind the battlements on his own turret, as the door opened and two men came through.

"It's a cold place for guard duty," one of them said. "How long do we have to stay here?"

"From moonrise to sun-up," said the other. "We're late tonight — the moon's been up an hour. But that's because we had to take over from the old guard."

"It's a long time till the sun rises," grumbled the first man.

"So it is, Galor," said the second. "But you'd better not let Soluken find you sleeping. He said that he needed a special watch kept on this tower, and I shouldn't be surprised if he comes up himself later to make sure his orders are being carried out. It would be just like him, to keep a watch on us. If he doesn't come himself, he'll send Tigman, and he's just as bad."

"I'm not planning to sleep," said Galor. "It's too cold."

He pulled his cloak around him, and stared out towards the mountains.

Nicholas moved down through the opening to the steps again, and pulled the stone softly back into place over his head. There was no way out for him that way, while the guards were there. He groped his way back down the steps to the passage, and moved along it.

As he passed the holes in the stone carving, he looked into the room where the Alarkin was. The Alarkin was sitting on his bed, gazing into the fire. There was no point in telling the Alarkin that the roof of the tower was guarded. Nicholas moved along the passage into the darkness beyond, feeling his way with one foot.

It was a good thing that he moved so carefully. The steps leading down were just past the carving.

Halfway down, there was another stone carving in the wall, with light showing through it. Nicholas stopped to look quickly through the holes.

He was looking into the room below the Alarkin's. Gunrun was sitting at a wooden table, eating his supper.

Nicholas went on quickly, groping his way downwards.

The passage turned sharply to the right, and stairs led on down through the wall of the tower.

Nicholas followed the stairs down past two more big rooms, and finally came to a stone wall at the bottom of the steps.

There was a stone carving in the wall here, too, but there was no door. Light shone in through the holes in the carving.

Nicholas looked through it, and saw that he was looking out of the tower, into a narrow lane. A lantern hung on a bracket on a wall on the opposite side of the lane, throwing light into the secret passage.

"There must be some way out," Nicholas muttered to himself. "There has to be."

He ran his fingers carefully over all the

holes and shapes in the carving. At one end, near one of the largest holes, his fingers touched a metal bolt, going down into the stone.

Nicholas pulled it. The bolt came upwards, out of the stone. At the same time, he felt the carving move.

Nicholas pushed against one end of the carving. The whole carved panel of stone turned slowly, on a bar going down through its centre. One end swung towards him, and the other end jutted out into the lane. There was just room for a man to creep through the opening on each side of the stone panel.

Nicholas put his head out through the opening, and looked quickly to left and right. The lane was empty. He slithered out as quickly as he could, and swung the carving back into place behind him. It fitted against the wall.

He slipped his hand into the hole at one end of the carving, and found that he could just push the bolt back into place.

Nicholas took another quick look along the lane. He thought he could see an opening in the walls of the houses in front of him, a few metres along to his left.

He walked quickly towards it, and found himself at the top of a flight of steps, leading down into the streets of the city.

He began to make his way down, as quickly as he could. The steps ended in a street. Nicholas looked left and right. There was no one about. He went on, into the city.

Lanterns hung at the corners of some of the streets, and there were lighted windows in many of the houses. The moon was up, and the city was flooded with moonlight.

Nicholas didn't know his way, but if he went steadily downwards, he knew he was bound to come down to the sea.

As he came to each corner, he stopped and listened, and then looked around the corner, to make sure that the way was clear, before going on.

At first, the streets seemed to be empty, but as he came towards the centre of the city, he began to see people, walking along past the houses.

The first time he saw them, he dodged into a darkened doorway, and waited until they had passed. But as he went on, into the city, there were so many people that he decided he would do better to walk openly through the streets as if he had every right to be there.

"After all," he thought, "I look like a citizen of Ramir myself."

At first, his heart beat wildly whenever he met anyone, but he soon realised that no one was looking at him. The people of Ramir were walking about their city at night as if nothing was wrong.

"They can't know what's happened," Nicholas muttered to himself. "But of course — Soluken won't have told them yet."

He came out into a big square, with a large building at one side. He stood for a moment, gazing at it. He recognised that building. It was the great house, where the Council of Ramir met. He remembered the way he had once gone with Captain Harken, a long time ago, across the square and down towards the sea.

He was just going to step out into the square, when a party of guards marched into it. They halted. The group broke up, and began to question the people in the square.

Nicholas dodged into a patch of black shadow. He thought for a moment that he could hide there, but then he remembered that his white shirt would show up, even in the dark.

He looked around quickly. There was an open window in a house near him. The room on the other side of the window was dark.

In a moment, he had slipped quickly through the window.

He found himself standing in the darkness in a little room. He could just see a door on the far side of it, with a crack of light around it.

As he watched it, the crack widened. The door was beginning to open.

Nicholas looked round wildly, but there was nowhere to hide. He put his hand on the side of the window, to climb back through, when the door was flung back, and a boy, carrying a lantern, came in.

Chapter 2
Escape from the city

For a moment, the boy stared at Nicholas in shocked surprise. Then his face brightened.

"Nicholas!" he cried. "Nicholas! You've come back!"

He limped quickly across the room, and at the same moment Nicholas recognised him.

"Haldur!" he cried. "Haldur!"

Haldur, the boy whose father had turned traitor, in order to save his son from the wolf men — and who had died, saving both Haldur and Nicholas from a sea monster! Haldur, who had gone with Nicholas and Captain Rasha into the mountains!

Haldur had proved that he was completely to be trusted. And now, here he was, in the City of Ramir.

"Nicholas," said Haldur, stopping just in front of him, and looking so happy that it was almost as if the sun was shining on his face. "Nicholas! Where have you come from?"

"I've only just come through the ring," said Nicholas.

Haldur nodded. "Captain Harken told me about that," he said. "I don't understand, but I know it's all right. Are you looking for Captain Harken? Barnabas said Captain Harken had adopted you as his son. But Captain Harken's on *The Silver Dolphin*. *The Silver Dolphin* is in the Sea Road, and they're sailing at first light."

"I've got to get to Captain Harken before the ship sails," said Nicholas. "Can you help me, Haldur? It's very important. He mustn't sail. You know that the Alarkin is King of Ramir?"

Haldur nodded. "Yes," he said. "Soluken is the Regent, until the Alarkin is old enough to rule by himself."

"Soluken's a traitor," said Nicholas. "He has made the Alarkin a prisoner, and shut him up in a tower. He's going to try to make the Alarkool king. I've got to find Captain Harken before he sails, and tell him."

"Can't you tell the guards?" asked Haldur quickly. "They'd free the Alarkin."

Nicholas shook his head. "They're Soluken's men," he said. "Soluken has replaced all the old guards with his own men tonight. They'd put me in prison, too, if they knew I was here. I've got to get to *The Silver Dolphin* without the guards knowing."

"The gates are all shut," said Haldur. "They shut them at sunset."

"Then I'll have to go over the wall," said Nicholas. "Could you get me a rope, Haldur?"

Haldur nodded. "Of course I can," he said. "This is Captain Harken's sister's house. Captain Harken keeps some of his things here. There's some of the ship's gear.

"Wait here a minute. I'll go and get a rope now. And I know where you can use the rope, too."

"The rope will have to be thick enough to hold me, and long enough to drop over the wall," said Nicholas.

Haldur nodded. "I know," he said.

Then he was gone, taking the lantern with him.

Nicholas turned back to the window and looked out into the square. The guards had formed up again, and were marching away.

In a few minutes, Haldur was back with a coil of rope, and two dark jackets, thrown over one arm.

"Here you are," he said, putting down the lantern. "Here's a jacket, Nicholas. It will be harder to see, than your white shirt. It's big enough for you. It's not mine."

He put down the rope and handed the jacket to Nicholas. Nicholas put it on.

"That was brilliant, Haldur," he said. "Thanks. Let me have the rope."

"I'm coming too," said Haldur, handing the rope to Nicholas, and putting on the other jacket. "I know the city better than you do. There's a dark lane going down to the Sea Road, and a place where we can climb over the wall. The guards would never let you out through the sea gate. I'll show you the way."

"Won't they miss you?" asked Nicholas.

Haldur shook his head. "Everyone thinks I've gone to bed," he said. "Come on."

The two boys clambered out of the window again, into the square. Nicholas carried the coil of rope under his jacket. The jacket didn't hide it very well, but it was better than nothing.

They moved out of the shadows into the light, and crossed the square.

They went into a narrow street on the far side. They turned down another street, and from there they went through an archway into a narrow lane.

It was dark in the lane. There were no lanterns on the houses, and, although the moon was high above the roof-tops, the lane itself was in shadow.

At the end of the lane there was another archway, with a wooden gate.

Haldur opened the gate softly, and they slipped through it into a dark courtyard. There were houses to the left and right of them, but the other side of the courtyard was a blank wall.

Nicholas caught his breath. It was the great outer wall, which ran around the City of Ramir.

"This way," whispered Haldur.

He led the way to a corner between the wall and one of the houses. The corner was in deep shadow. It was only as they came to it, that Nicholas saw there were steps there. The steps led up, on to the wall.

Haldur crept softly up the steps, with Nicholas at his heels. When he got to the top, he looked both ways.

"No one here," he whispered.

The boys climbed up on to the top of the

wall. The moon was shining down, and across the wall, Nicholas saw the sea.

The wall was wide enough for three men to walk abreast. There were battlements on the far side of it.

"We'll tie the rope around one of the battlements, and slide down the other side," whispered Haldur. "Then we'll be on the quay. I've got a little rowing boat of my own tied up there. Captain Harken gave it to me, so that I could go fishing. We'll row out to *The Silver Dolphin.*"

"We can't both go, Haldur," Nicholas said softly. "I wish you could come with me — but I must leave you in the city, so that I can come back again the same way. I'll have to come back, to rescue the Alarkin — or the buccaneers will. We'll need someone to drop a rope over the wall. And we can't leave this rope here, for Soluken's guards to find."

"But —" began Haldur.

"You must take the rope, and go home, so that no one knows anyone has left the city, Haldur," said Nicholas. "And then, when I want to come back — do you know that big rock, a hundred metres or so along the Sea Road? I saw it from the tower."

"The Dragon Rock," said Haldur. "I know it."

"I'll light a fire on the Dragon Rock, when I want to come back. Watch for it. When you see a fire there, come down here at midnight with the rope. Can you do that?"

"I'll do it," said Haldur.

"Do you have owls in Ramir?"

"Yes," said Haldur in surprise. "You can hear them sometimes near the city. They live in holes on the cliffs, and in one of the towers."

"Then I'll hoot like an owl, when I'm near the wall," said Nicholas. "When you hear me, hoot back, if the way is clear, and drop the rope over the wall. Can you hoot?"

For answer, Haldur lifted his hands to his mouth. A long, mournful cry, like that of an owl, echoed against the mountainside.

"Softly!" whispered Nicholas.

They both listened for a moment, but there was no sound, except the waves breaking against the stone quay.

"I'll go now," whispered Nicholas. "Where did you say the boat was?"

"You'll drop down at the very end of the quay, where the quay ends and the mountain begins," said Haldur. "The boat's tied up there. The oars are on the quay, just under the wall. *The Silver Dolphin* is moored against the left side of the Sea Road, a long way beyond the Dragon Rock."

"Fine," said Nicholas. "I'll get there as soon as I can. You get yourself home safely. Remember, we'll need you. If you're not there, we may not be able to get back into the city."

"I'll be there," said Haldur.

Nicholas had been tying the rope around one of the battlements while he was speaking. Now he dropped the free end down over the wall.

He looked out between the battlements. He could see the quay below him, and the Sea Road of Ramir stretching out in front of him in the moonlight. Boats were tied up to the quay, but no one was in sight.

He smiled at Haldur in the moonlight.

"I'll be back," he said cheerfully.

He climbed quickly between the battlements, and slid down the rope.

As soon as he reached the ground, he looked up. Haldur was looking over the wall.

Nicholas waved his hand, and then looked along the quay. It was still empty.

He looked down by the wall. A little farther along, he saw a pair of oars. He picked them up, and went to the end of the quay.

A little rowing boat was there, fastened by a rope to a ring at his feet. It was bobbing up and down on the waves.

Nicholas put the oars on the edge of the quay, climbed down into the boat, and lifted the oars in after him. He untied the rope, and dropped it into the boat. Then he sat down, and lifted each oar into its rowlock.

With a long, strong pull, Nicholas sent the little boat out into the waves.

Chapter 3
In the Sea Road of Ramir

After his first few pulls on the oars, Nicholas guessed that the tide must have turned. It was beginning to go out.

That meant that he must hurry. The outgoing tide would carry him with it, but it also meant that *The Silver Dolphin* would sail.

But there was very little wind. Nicholas was enough of a sailor now, to know that *The Silver Dolphin* couldn't sail down the Sea Road unless there was a good wind from the north. The long boat would have to tow her out, until she reached the open sea. That gave him a chance to reach her, before she left.

He settled down to row as hard and as steadily as he could. His own father had taught him to row years ago, and he had had some practice, too, with the buccaneers. The little boat travelled swiftly along on the outgoing tide.

The moon was shining down, but it was moving towards the west. Part of the Sea Road lay in shadow. In the east, the sky looked a little paler. Dawn was not far away.

Nicholas rowed past Dragon Rock, and on, down the Sea Road. He passed one or two large fishing boats, anchored to the side. But there were no fighting ships of Ramir. He remembered that they had all sailed south — all of them, except for *The Silver Dolphin* and *The Blue Whale*. There might have been fishermen sleeping on the boats, but nobody was keeping watch. No one challenged him, as he rowed past.

Every now and then, he glanced over his shoulder, looking for *The Silver Dolphin.*

He began to be afraid that she might have sailed already.

On he went, down the dark Sea Road of Ramir, rowing as if his life depended on it.

Then, when his arms were aching with tiredness, he looked over his shoulder and saw the ship.

She was a long way ahead of him, moving out from the dark shadows by the side, into the Sea Road. The long boat was towing her.

Nicholas tossed off his jacket, and redoubled his efforts. He was rowing harder than he had ever rowed in his life.

When he looked back again, he saw *The Blue Whale* being towed out behind *The Silver Dolphin.* He set his teeth, and rowed on.

The tide was running more swiftly now. It was helping him to travel faster, but it was helping the ships, too.

When he glanced back again, he saw that they were setting one of the sails on *The Blue Whale.* The wind was a little stronger. If they once used the sails, he would never be able to catch them.

Nicholas quickly shipped the oars. He stood up, balancing himself in the boat, and shouted as loudly as he could.

The sound echoed against the cliffs. There

was no reply. The ships were still moving away.

Nicholas pulled off his white shirt. He tied it to one of the oars, lifted the oar up, and waved it like a flag. Then he shouted again, as loudly as before.

For a moment, nothing happened. And then he saw the boat, which was towing *The Blue Whale,* drop the tow rope, and turn towards him. Were they just going back on board, or had they seen him?

He waved the oar to and fro, shouting until his voice cracked.

The long boat passed the ship, and continued rowing towards him. He had been seen.

Nicholas's knees suddenly felt very weak. He sat down hard, and lowered the oar. With shaking hands, he untied his shirt, and put it on.

Then he put the oar back in the rowlock, and rowed rather jerkily towards the oncoming long boat.

"Who's there? And what do you want?"

The cry from the long boat carried a long way across the water.

Nicholas tried to shout, but his voice came out as a croak. He swallowed hard, and tried again.

"It's me, Nicholas," he called. "Nicholas Strange. I've got to see Captain Harken."

"Nicholas! Young Nick!" shouted the man steering the long boat. "Hang on a minute, Nick. We'll be with you."

It was Spider's voice. Nicholas was sure of that. Spider was a sailor on *The Blue Whale*. Nicholas had last seen him when they had both been looking for the Sea-king's treasure.

He pulled slowly towards the long boat. His arms felt so tired and shaky, that he did little more than keep Haldur's boat steady.

The long boat swept alongside.

"Have you got a painter, Nick?" shouted Spider.

"Yes," called Nicholas. He knew that meant a rope, fastened to the bows.

"Throw it across."

Nicholas shipped his oars, and went to the bows of the little rowing boat. He picked up the end of the rope which Haldur had used to fasten the boat to the quay, and tossed it over to waiting hands, held out from the stern of the long boat.

"We'll soon have you aboard *The Blue Whale,* Nick," Spider called. "We can signal Captain Harken from there."

The long boat turned, and sped back towards the big ship. There were twelve men at the oars, and she seemed to fly over the water.

When they reached the ship, Spider and the buccaneers waited alongside, while Nick climbed up the rope ladder, which hung down over the side. Then they rowed back to the bows of *The Blue Whale,* to pick up the tow rope, while the little rowing boat was hauled on deck.

Martin Quinn was on the deck, waiting.

"By all the stars, I might have known it!" he cried, as Nicholas climbed on to the deck. "The whole world is washed in silver moonlight tonight. Have you come to look for the Sea-king's treasure again, Nicholas? I don't think we'll find it this time. It's too deep down, at the bottom of the sea."

Nicholas shook his head.

"It's not that," he said. "The Alarkin's in danger. I've got to see Captain Harken."

Martin Quinn's welcoming smile faded.

"The Alarkin in danger!" he exclaimed. "Why, we only left him yesterday morning, in Ramir. What's happened, Nick?"

"Soluken's turned traitor," said Nicholas. "He's put the Alarkin in prison. He's trying to make the Alarkool King of Ramir."

Martin Quinn turned, and called up to a sailor who was standing on the poop deck.

"Signal *The Silver Dolphin,*" he called. "Use the lantern. Send this signal to Captain Harken. 'Urgent news. Am sending messenger across to you'."

He shouted orders for the long boat. Again, the tow rope was dropped, and Spider brought the boat alongside.

"Take Nicholas over to *The Silver Dolphin* right away, Spider," called Martin Quinn. "I'm coming, too." He turned to another buccaneer, who had just come up from below. "I'm leaving you in charge, Cal. There's enough wind to steer now. Move slowly down the Sea Road. Follow *The Silver Dolphin.*"

"Aye, aye, Captain," said Cal.

"Down you go, Nicholas."

Nicholas climbed down the rope ladder into the long boat, followed by Martin Quinn.

The boat moved away from the ship. *The Silver Dolphin* was waiting for them, and they rowed across to her. Nicholas felt a surge of happiness, as he saw the great carved silver dolphin under the bows of the big ship.

"Follow us up on deck, Spider," said Martin Quinn, as he gripped the rope ladder hanging down the ship's side. "The men can take the long boat back. I don't know how long we shall be."

Nicholas climbed up the rope ladder after Martin Quinn, and Spider followed him.

Captain Harken was standing on the deck, waiting for them.

"Nicholas!" cried Captain Harken, as Nicholas clambered over the ship's side. "Is this your news, Martin?"

"It's only the beginning of it," said Martin Quinn. "Nicholas is just the messenger. There's more news to come, and it's urgent."

"I'm very glad to see you, Nicholas," said Captain Harken. "Come into the great cabin. You too, Spider. Downalong, find Barnabas and Tom Gold, and ask them to join us there at once. Take over the ship yourself for the time being. The course is south, down the Sea Road. Signal *The Blue Whale,* to keep with us."

"Aye, aye, Captain," said Downalong.

Nicholas followed the others into the great cabin. Captain Harken sat down at the head of the table, with Martin Quinn beside him. They were soon joined by Barnabas and Tom Gold.

"Now, Nicholas, let's have your story," said Captain Harken. "Sit down, boy, and tell us your news."

Nicholas sat down. Everyone was watching him. He drew a deep breath, and began.

"I — I came through the ring tonight," he said. "And I found myself in a secret passage, in a big tower — the tower in the city wall, overlooking the mountains."

Captain Harken nodded. "I know it," he said. "I didn't know it had a secret passage. Well?"

Nicholas told them what had happened. He found that he could repeat most of the things Soluken and the Alarkool had said. He told them how he had spoken to the Alarkin, and how he had made his way down through the darkened city.

When he told them about Haldur, Barnabas Brandy banged his right fist down on the table.

"Who'd have believed it?" he cried.

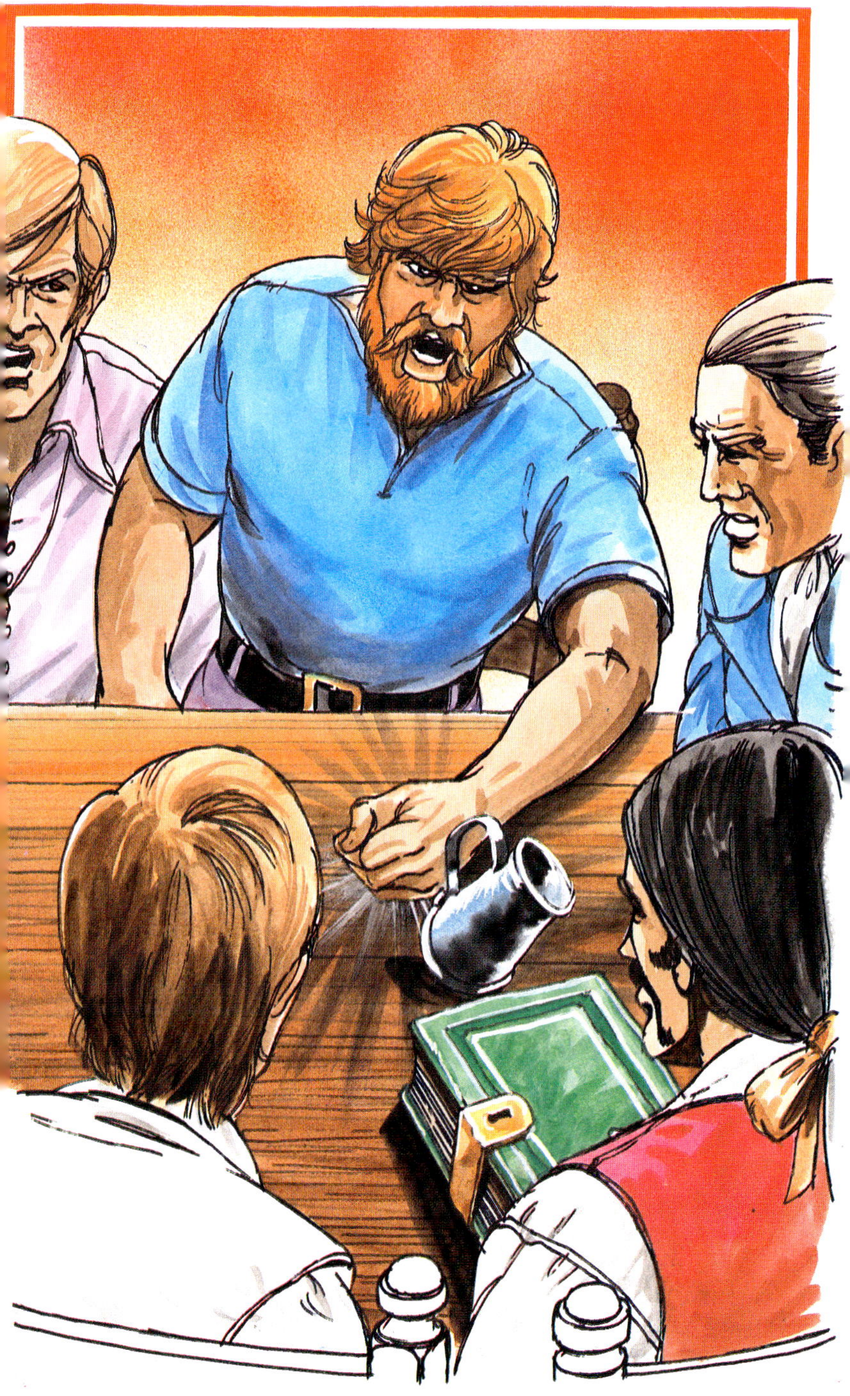

"You're sure he'll keep quiet about it, Nick?"

"Of course I'm sure," said Nicholas.

"I trust Haldur, too," said Captain Harken quietly. "He's a good lad. I've got to know him well, these last few months. Haldur won't say anything. Go on, Nicholas."

Nicholas told them about his escape over the wall of Ramir, and how Spider had finally seen him, waving from the rowing boat.

"It's a good thing you have sharp eyes, Spider," said Captain Harken. "Well, Nicholas — this time you really have come here to help us to save Ramir. I've always had doubts about Soluken. Now we know what he is — a traitor to Ramir, a man who wants power for himself at all costs.

"What we have to do, is to see that he never gets that power."

"We'll see to that," said Barnabas Brandy. "We'll sail south, and find the fleet. The buccaneers of Ramir will never stand for this. They'll be against Soluken to a man.

"We'll fill the Sea Road with the fighting ships of Ramir. We'll storm the city, and hang Soluken like the traitor that he is!"

"Well, that would be one way to do it," said Captain Harken. "What do you think, Martin?"

"If we have to storm the walls of Ramir, it will be a fearful battle," said Martin Quinn quietly. "Three or four companies could hold those walls against an army. I'd sooner find some other way, if we can.''

Captain Harken nodded. ''So would I,'' he said. ''The people of Ramir are the ones who will suffer, if we have to take the city by storm.

''And remember that our own families are among them. They'll be seized as hostages, the moment Soluken knows that we're moving against him.

''And what about the Alarkin, Barnabas? How long do you think the Alarkin would remain alive, if the buccaneers were battering at the gates of the city?''

''It's my belief that it wouldn't only be the Alarkin — it might be the Alarkool as well,'' said Martin Quinn. ''Soluken wants to rule Ramir himself. I've always thought that. I wouldn't give much for the chances of any son of the Lord of Ramir, if he got in Soluken's way.''

''Nor would I, Martin,'' said Captain Harken. ''Whatever we do, we must do quickly. We mustn't give Soluken a chance to harm the Alarkin — or anyone else.

''Soluken holds the city. His own men have disarmed the guard, and taken over.

''He's formed a new Council of Ramir, which will pass any laws he cares to make.''

''He had no right to do that!'' cried Barnabas Brandy. ''The Council of Ramir is elected by the people. And the elected Council chose the Alarkin as their king.''

''I think the elected Council is probably in

prison," said Captain Harken. "There are some men and women on the Council of Ramir who would never have allowed this to happen, if they had had a chance to resist. It must have all happened very quickly.

"Soluken had no right to do what he has done — but he's done it, nonetheless. It was well planned. He had been carefully putting his own men into important posts ever since the Lord of Ramir fell ill. He already had some of his friends on the elected Council of Ramir. It was they who made him regent. You may be sure that every member of the new Council is one of his own men.

"We can take it that he holds the City of Ramir. Many people won't like it — but Soluken's men will be armed, and they'll see to it that no one protests too much.

"What we must do, is to find some way to take over the city again with as little fighting as possible. The people in the city are the people of Ramir. They're not enemies. We can't attack them.

"Whatever we do, we must keep our actions secret.

"We've started on our journey to Ikroon, to try to bring back the Sea-king's treasure — or at any rate, that's what Soluken will think. We must be near the open sea by now.

"I suggest that we sail eastwards, as if we were setting out across the ocean towards Ikroon. As soon as we are well out to sea, beyond the sight of the little ships that sail up and down the coast, we'll change course.

"The fleet should know what has happened. I'm certain that the buccaneers will stand by the Alarkin.

"Martin, you must sail south, and find the fleet. Captain Yarrel is in command. He's a true man, and a friend of mine — that's one reason why Soluken sent him out of the way.

"You must tell Captain Yarrel what has happened. Ask Captain Yarrel to return with the whole fleet, and meet us farther down the coast, in Hidden Harbour.

"You remember Hidden Harbour, Martin? Captain Rohni hid *The Silver Dolphin* there, when we were both ship's boys?"

"Of course I remember," said Martin Quinn. "I'll never forget. There were half a dozen pirate ships looking for us. We went into Hidden Harbour, and sent a message to the High Captain. Ten fighting ships sailed out of the Sea Road. They sank four of the pirates' ships, and took the other two captive."

"I knew you'd remember," said Captain Harken. "Well, I'll hide *The Silver Dolphin* in Hidden Harbour now. I'll leave her there, with a crew on board.

"I'll take ten men from *The Silver Dolphin* and go back across the mountains to Brenan's house, on the high land above the city."

"Do you think Brenan will help us?" asked Tom Gold. "He's a wild man, so they say.

And his house is more like a fortress than a house, up there on the mountain."

"That's one reason why it will be a good place to make our headquarters," said Captain Harken. "The house can be defended — if we have to defend it. But I hope we won't have to.

"Brenan was a friend of the Lord of Ramir. He lives a strange, rough life, up there on the mountain. But he's a true man. Soluken could never buy him. The Lord of Ramir was glad to have Brenan living on the mountain. He said that he was one of the best guards Ramir had. He'll help us, all right.

"The first thing we have to do, is to try to smuggle the Alarkin out of prison.

"We'll try and find out what is happening in the city, too, and how many men Soluken has.

"When you come back with the fleet, we'll smuggle some of the buccaneers secretly back into the city at night. They can go in by the same way that Nicholas came out. We'll catch Soluken's men unawares.

"You must come ahead of the fleet, Martin, and get a message through to me at Brenan's house. Then, if we're lucky, we'll take Soluken's men prisoner before they know what's happening."

Captain Harken paused, and looked at the men around the table.

"The captain's right," said Tom Gold.

"It's the best way to take the city, with as

little bloodshed as possible," said Martin Quinn.

"I'd like to shed Soluken's blood," said Barnabas Brandy. "I'd like to fight him myself, cutlass against cutlass. But you're right, Francis. It's a better plan than storming the walls. Too many people besides Soluken will get hurt, if we try to do it that way. I can see that."

"Spider?" asked Captain Harken.

"I agree with you, Captain Harken," said Spider. "I'd like to try to rescue the Alarkin, too, before any fighting starts. I don't trust Soluken."

"Then we're all agreed," said Captain Harken, pushing back his chair, and getting up. "We'll sail eastwards now, and turn back for the coast as soon as it's dark this evening."

He looked at Nicholas.

"When did you last have something to eat?" he asked.

"I can't remember," said Nicholas.

Captain Harken laughed. "You'll find Halek below," he said. "Ask him to find some food for you. Then you'd better get some rest. You've been up most of the night already. It's almost daylight now. There's a bed waiting for you in the starboard cabin, Nicholas. We keep it there for you, these days.

"We'd all better get as much rest today as

we can, on *The Silver Dolphin.* We'll be up tonight again.''

The meeting broke up. Nicholas went off to find Halek.

Martin Quinn went back to *The Blue Whale,* but Spider asked if he could stay on board *The Silver Dolphin.*

"We're all in for an exciting time," he said cheerfully. "It's going to be dangerous, too. If there's going to be danger, I'd like to be on the same ship as young Nicholas."

Captain Harken laughed.

"It's surprising how well Nicholas can take care of himself," he said. "But you can keep an eye on him, if you like."

"It's not so much that I want to look after *him,*" said Spider. "It's more that I'd be glad to know that he was looking after *me!* Nick always seems to turn up just when he's needed. It was Nick who rescued me in Ikroon — not the other way about. If Nick's going to be on *The Silver Dolphin,* I'd like to be on *The Silver Dolphin* too."

So Spider stayed, and Barnabas found a spare hammock for him below deck.

Chapter 4
Brenan's house

Nicholas slept all day, and when at last he woke up, it was dark again outside. He got up, and went into the great cabin.

Captain Harken was there, poring over a map. He looked up and saw Nicholas, and smiled at him cheerfully.

"We'll be in before long, Nick," he said. "How would you like to slip down below decks, and bring me some hot soup? You might get some for yourself, at the same time."

The door opened, and Barnabas Brandy looked in.

"The long boat's away, Francis," he said.

"Shut that door, Barnabas!" said Captain Harken. "We mustn't show a gleam of light, if we can help it."

Barnabas came in and shut the door behind him.

"I'll come up on deck," said Captain Harken, rolling up the map. "Bring the soup up there, Nick. And get Halek to bring some for Barnabas. But be sure you don't show a light. Find your way in the dark.

"I'll blow this lantern out before you open that door, Barnabas. You don't know who may be up there, on the cliffs."

"There's no one living for miles along this coast," said Barnabas.

"But there may be shepherds on the hills," said Captain Harken. "They wouldn't mean to do us any harm, but they might spread a tale about *The Silver Dolphin* anchoring in Hidden Harbour. And Soluken's men will have their ears open, listening to every story."

Captain Harken blew out the lantern, and the darkness closed in on them. Then Barnabas opened the door — an oblong of dark grey against the dark sky.

They went out on deck. The sky was covered in black clouds, and it was almost as dark outside as it had been in the cabin. The silver lantern on the bows of the ship had been wrapped in a dark cloak.

"The weather's been kind to us," said Captain Harken. "The moon's at the full tonight. Without those clouds, it would have been almost as light as day."

Nicholas waited until his eyes were a little more used to the darkness. Then he made his way carefully over to the hatch that led below.

The hatch was closed. He opened it, and a square of faint light showed at his feet.

He went down to the galley. The galley was lit by the red ashes of a fire, set on a large square stone. The portholes were closed, and everything smelt of smoke.

The cook was just ladling out two large mugs of soup, when Halek loomed up out of the darkness beside him.

"Can I give you a hand, Nick?" he asked.

"Captain Harken said that you should take soup up for Barnabas," said Nicholas. "They're both on deck. We're just going into the harbour."

In the end, Nicholas took soup for Captain Harken, and Halek carried some up for Barnabas. Then Halek went back down, and came up with a mug for Nicholas and one for himself.

Once he was on deck, Nicholas didn't want to go down again. The long boat was slowly towing the ship towards the great black cliffs, that loomed up ahead of them out of the darkness.

Barnabas was at the wheel, and Captain Harken was in command.

Nicholas went forward to watch. He could hear waves breaking, and as the ship moved slowly forwards in the darkness, he saw the waves breaking in a rush of white water ahead of them.

"Hard a-starboard, Tom!" Captain Harken called to Tom Gold, who was in the long boat.

The long boat turned sharply to one side, and the ship followed.

Nicholas looked down. They were sliding through a narrow channel of dark water. Waves broke on the rocks on either side of them.

Then they were through, and into the dark water ahead. They seemed to be moving straight towards the towering cliffs, but as they reached them, they swung to the right again. Nicholas saw that they were making their way up a narrow channel of water with high cliffs on either side of them. It was like the Sea Road of Ramir, but much smaller. The channel soon opened out into a wide circle of water, with cliffs rising up on every side.

It was a perfect secret harbour. There was room in it for three or four ships, but it was completely hidden from the sea by towering cliffs, and there was only one entrance: the narrow channel, through which they had just come.

"Lower away!" cried Captain Harken.

The anchor chain rattled down into the sea.

The long boat came back. Tom Gold and the other buccaneers climbed on board.

"Light the lanterns," said Captain Harken. "We can't be seen from the sea now — or from the land, unless someone is peering over the cliffs looking down into the harbour. And if they are, they'll see us anyway, so we may as well have some light.

"Set a watch on deck, Barnabas. I'm going to get some sleep."

The black clouds overhead were split by a flash of lightning. The crash of thunder sounded directly overhead. It was so loud, that for a moment Nicholas thought the cliffs were falling. The skies opened, and the rain poured down in sheets.

"Everyone under cover, except the watch!" cried Captain Harken.

The buccaneers disappeared down the hatch, and Captain Harken moved swiftly into the great cabin, followed by Nicholas. Halek had already lit the lantern there, and the cabin looked warm and dry and welcoming. The lightning forked down and the thunder crashed outside.

"We'll have to start for Brenan's house soon after midnight," said Captain Harken. "Let's hope the storm is over by then. Wake me at two bells, Nicholas."

He went into the port cabin to sleep.

Nicholas passed the time looking at the maps and charts on the table, or staring out of the window in the starboard cabin.

At first, a flash of lightning lit the sky every few minutes. The crash of the thunder echoed from the cliffs, while the rain poured down. But the time between flashes of lightning and rolls of thunder gradually grew longer and longer. The storm was moving away, across the mountains.

Nicholas heard the rain falling for some time after the last echoes of thunder had died away. But in the end, even the rain stopped. The black clouds overhead parted, and the moon shone down.

Nicholas went out on deck. Two buccaneers were keeping watch. The lantern shone on the bows of the ship. He looked around at the Hidden Harbour, but there was not much for him to see. There was the narrow channel, leading to the open sea, and the ring of towering cliffs all around the ship. Water was pouring down them, splashing over the rocks in high waterfalls.

As soon as he heard two bells being struck, Nicholas called Captain Harken. A meal was set on the table in the great cabin. Nicholas wasn't sure whether it was an early breakfast or a late supper, but he was glad to have it. He had learnt to eat whenever he was given the chance, when he sailed with the buccaneers. He never knew how long it might be to the next meal.

As soon as they had eaten, Captain Harken called everyone on deck. The silver lantern on the bows of the ship was shining brightly. The whole deck was lit by lanterns swinging from the rigging.

"I'm leaving Barnabas and Tom Gold here in charge of the ship," said Captain Harken. "I'm taking ten men with me, and going across the mountains to Brenan's house. The rest of you will stay here, and wait for us — and for the fleet."

"You'll need more than ten men, Francis," protested Barnabas. "You'll have to defend Brenan's house, if Soluken once knows you are there."

"He won't know," said Captain Harken. "Everything we do must be kept secret. Ten men is really too many, but I want to be sure that we can defend ourselves, if we do run into trouble.

"And all we are going to do is to try to find out what is happening in the city. And to rescue the Alarkin, if we can."

"*All* you're going to do!" cried Barnabas. "That's work for a company, not ten men."

"Ten is enough," said Captain Harken. "We shall work secretly.

"The rest of you will stay here, and get ready to retake the city. Keep to the ship, and don't let anyone see you here.

"Now, who will come with me? It will be dangerous — and a long, hard walk!"

Every buccaneer stepped forward to volunteer. Captain Harken chose Downalong Joe, Spider and seven others.

"Who's the tenth?" asked Barnabas.

"Nicholas, if he'll come," said Captain Harken.

"Of *course* I will," said Nicholas.

Barnabas laughed.

"Remember, you're a man, Nick," he said.

"Nicholas is one of us," said Captain Harken quietly. "And he knows the secret passage." He raised his voice again. "All right, men. We'll leave the ship in ten minutes time. Each man should bring a cutlass and a pistol with him. Wear your dark jackets. We mustn't be seen."

Ten minutes later, the party set out from the ship. The long boat ferried them across to a flat rock, and from there they started the long climb up the cliffs.

Steps had been cut in the side of the cliff, but it was hard going. The steps were worn with age, and the rock was wet and slippery. They had to use their hands, as well as their feet, to stop themselves falling.

Captain Harken led the way, with Nicholas behind him, followed by Spider. Downalong Joe came last. They wound their way slowly up the side of the high cliff.

Nicholas did his best to keep his mind on the climb, and not to think about the sheer drop to the sea on his right, but all the time he could hear the waves washing against the rocks.

They stopped for a few minutes, halfway up, to rest. They could see the ship below them, lit by the lanterns, in the middle of a ring of dark water. It was like climbing up the side of a great, wide well.

Nicholas was thankful when at last they reached the top, and climbed over the edge of the cliffs on to level ground. He found himself standing on a wide, flat land, covered with heather and rocks. The moon was fully out now, and they could see clearly. The land reminded Nicholas of the moors at home.

"This way," said Captain Harken, moving off along the edge of the cliffs.

The others followed him, walking in single file. It was rough going. Nicholas could see that Captain Harken was following some

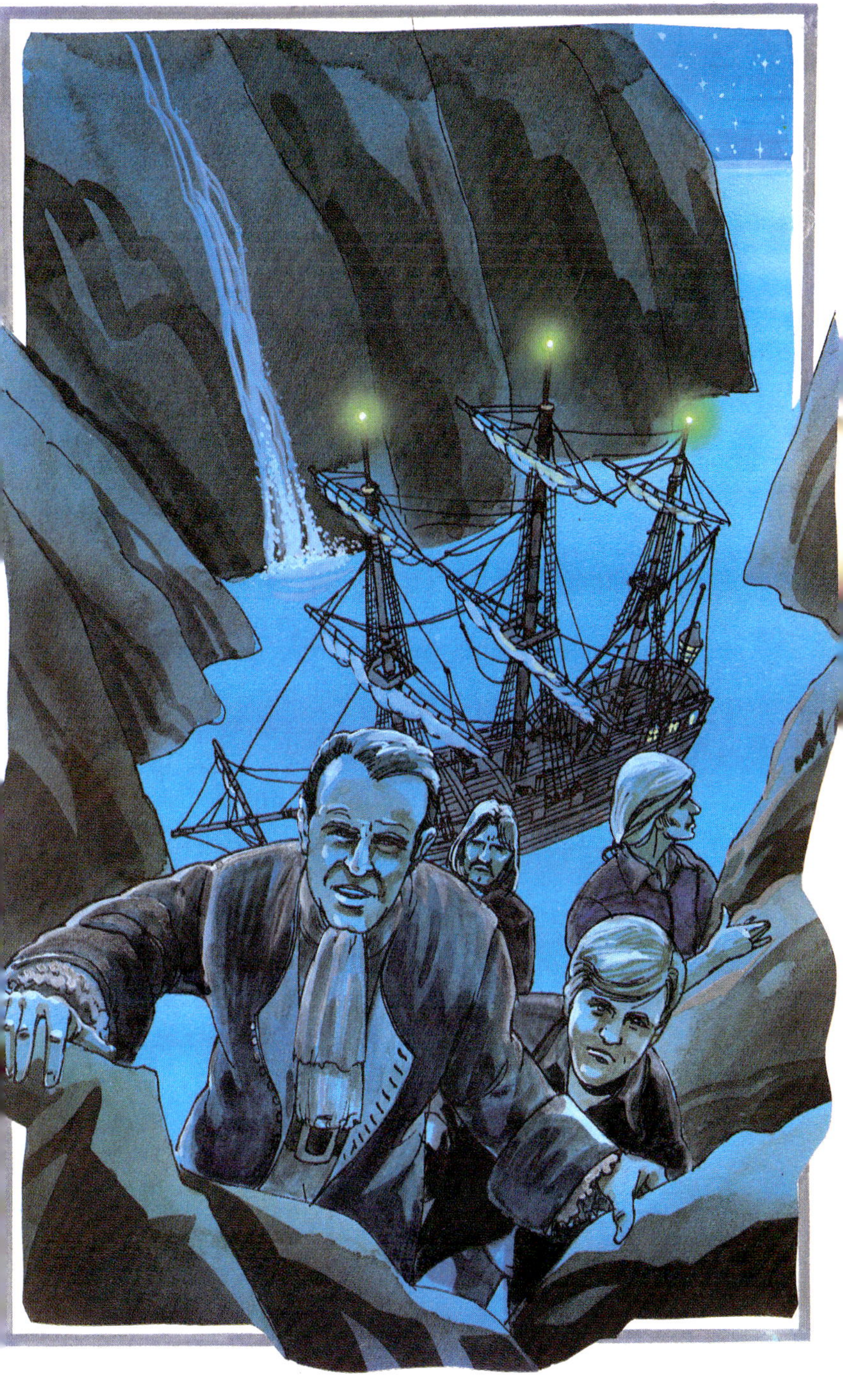

kind of path, but it was little more than a sheep track. Several times, Nicholas stumbled over a stone, and once he caught his foot in a root, and fell. But he picked himself up again quickly, and went on.

The sky in the east was just beginning to get light, when at last Captain Harken halted, and pointed across the moor.

"Brenan's house," he said.

They could see the house, a kilometre away from them. It was built near a pile of rocks, and it almost looked part of the rock itself. There was a stone wall all around it. They could just see the dark roofs of buildings rising above the wall.

By the time they reached the house, the light was stronger. A deep ditch had been dug all around the house, outside the wall. There was no water in the ditch, but Nicholas saw that it made the wall seem much higher.

They walked along the edge of the ditch until they saw a great gate, covered by a drawbridge. There was a small stone tower on each side of the gate.

On their side of the ditch, a wooden post had been driven into the ground. A horn hung from an iron peg, on the side of the post.

Captain Harken lifted the horn to his lips, and blew.

At once, a man appeared on one of the towers by the gate.

"Who calls?" he cried. "And what do you want?"

"I am Francis Harken, from *The Silver Dolphin*. We've come to ask Brenan for help."

The man disappeared without a word. A few minutes later, the drawbridge rattled down slowly on two long chains, and one of the biggest men Nicholas had ever seen strode across the drawbridge to meet them. He had thick black hair and a long black beard.

"Francis!" he cried in a deep voice. "You're very welcome. But what are you doing here? I heard that *The Silver Dolphin* had sailed for Ikroon. You weren't driven back on the coast in last night's storm?"

"No, Brenan, we anchored safely before the storm came. But there are strange things happening in the city, and we need your help. May we come in?"

"Come in and welcome. No one shall ever say that I kept Francis Harken and the men of *The Silver Dolphin* waiting at my door!"

He turned, and led the way back across the drawbridge, into a courtyard. Low buildings, with stone walls and stone-tiled roofs, stood all about them, inside the surrounding wall.

"It would be as well if the drawbridge were pulled up, Brenan," said Captain Harken. "I don't want anyone to know that we're here."

Brenan looked quickly at him, but he didn't ask any questions. He made a sign with his hand to one of his men. Nicholas heard the chains rattle, as the drawbridge was lifted back into place.

"Come into the hall," said Brenan. "Where did you leave the ship?"

"In Hidden Harbour," said Captain Harken.

"Then you've come a long way, and you must be hungry. Will your news wait, while we have breakfast?"

"We'll talk over breakfast," said Captain Harken. "We all need food and rest, and there's nothing to be done till evening. First, we must tell you what has happened, and plan our next move."

Brenan nodded, and led the way into one of the buildings. Nicholas followed Captain Harken through the door. He found himself standing in a long, wide room. There was a table down the centre of it. An immense fire was roaring cheerfully under a great stone chimney at one side. Nicholas looked up, and saw black rafters above his head, and the underside of the stone roof.

There were wooden chairs around the table. Brenan shouted some orders. Then he sat down at the table with the buccaneers, and some of Brenan's own men.

Nicholas thought that Brenan's men looked as tough and strong as anyone he had ever seen. They wore short tunics, with sleeveless leather jackets over them. Every man had a belt around his waist, with a long knife pushed into it.

Soon, men came hurrying in with great dishes of meat and fish and bread and fruit, which they put down on the table.

Nicholas suddenly felt very tired and very hungry. He was glad of the warmth and rest and food. He was sitting at the far end of the table, away from Captain Harken and Brenan. Everyone was talking together and he couldn't hear what was being said.

He watched a man bringing in a great jug of ale for the buccaneers. Someone had already set a drink of fruit juice and honey down for Nicholas.

The man leant forward to pour a drink for Downalong Joe, and Nicholas suddenly remembered him. He was Mori, one of the buccaneers who had sailed with Martin Quinn, when they had first found the Sea-king's treasure. He wondered what Mori could be doing there, in Brenan's house. Nicholas looked across at Spider, but Spider was busy talking to the man next to him.

Mori finished filling the drinking horns with ale, and left the room. Nicholas settled down to breakfast.

Chapter 5
Mori

After breakfast, the table was cleared. Brenan glanced around, and then crashed his fist down on the boards.

At once, there was silence. Everyone looked towards Brenan, listening.

"Captain Harken has told me what has happened," said Brenan, in his deep voice. "It is clear, what we must do. The Alarkin is the rightful King of Ramir. He is in danger. We must send men into the city, to rescue him.

"Then, when he is safe, we must take over the city. Captain Harken has said that we should do this with as little bloodshed as possible, and I agree with him — except that I think Soluken must die. We will not have traitors in Ramir.

"But first, we have to rescue the Alarkin. Well, Francis? Let us hear your plan."

"I think we should rescue the Alarkin as secretly as we can," said Captain Harken. "Nicholas can get back into the city tonight. If we send a man to light a fire on the Dragon Rock, Haldur, who lives with my sister, will drop a rope down over the wall. Four men should go with him — no more than that, or they will be discovered. I shall be one of them."

Mori came back into the room with another jug of ale. Brenan signed to him to go away, but Nicholas noticed that he went slowly, and left the door a little ajar behind him.

Captain Harken went on speaking. "We must make our way through the city to the old tower, that looks out on to the mountains. When we are there, Nicholas will show us the way to the roof of the tower, by a secret passage.

"Once on the roof, we must overcome the guard who will be there. We must do this as silently as we can. The guard mustn't have a chance to raise the alarm.

"We'll take a rope with us. We'll tie up the guards, and lower them to the ground. Then we'll climb down ourselves. The rope will drop down near the Alarkin's window. So the Alarkin can climb down too and escape with us.

"While we're doing all this, you must bring some men across the mountains, Brenan, to the foot of the tower. We'll join you, as soon as we can. And then we shall all make our way across the moor, back to your house.

"When Soluken finds the Alarkin gone, and a rope hanging down from the battlements, he will think that the guards have turned against him, and set the Alarkin free. He'll think they did it for gold.

"He thinks that the fighting ships are in the south, and that *The Silver Dolphin* and *The Blue Whale* have sailed for Ikroon. He will think that there is nothing the Alarkin can do, even if he is free.

"So we shall still have a chance to surprise him, and take the city."

There was silence for a moment. Then Spider spoke.

"You can't go into the city yourself, Captain Harken," he said. "You're too well known. You couldn't get to the tower, without someone recognising you."

Brenan nodded.

"*You* can't be one of that party, Francis," he said. "You'll do better to come with me to the foot of the tower, on the mountain side of the wall."

"The men who go into the city will be in the greatest danger," said Captain Harken quietly. "I can't send Nicholas, and men from my ship, into that kind of danger, unless I go myself."

"It'll be more dangerous for us if you come," said Spider. "I haven't been inside the City of Ramir for years — not since I was a boy. No one will recognise me there. But if you were there, none of us would be safe.

"I'll go with young Nick. I'd rather be with Nick, than with a whole shipful of buccaneers!

"We'll have to take two or three more with us, to make sure of the guards on the tower. But we'll all be a lot safer, if they are men who won't be recognised."

"He's right, Francis," growled Brenan.

"You know he is."

Captain Harken said nothing for a minute or two. Then he leant back in his chair.

"Very well," he said. "I don't like it, but I think perhaps you are right, Spider. And if I don't go myself, I'd like you to lead the party. Who will you take with you?"

"Jory, Spike and Jem," said Spider.

Captain Harken looked across at the three buccaneers, who were sitting together on the far side of the fire.

"Jory?" he asked.

"That's all right by me," said one of them. He was a red-haired man, with very blue eyes.

"Spike?"

A tall, dark-skinned buccaneer, nodded his head, without speaking.

"Jem?"

The third buccaneer grinned cheerfully. Nicholas had noticed him on board the ship, because he always looked so happy, even in the rain. He was a big, strong man, and Nicholas was glad that he was coming with them.

"I wouldn't miss it for anything," said Jem.

"All right, Spider," said Captain Harken. "When will be the best time to get into the city, Nicholas?"

"Midnight," said Nicholas. "Haldur will be waiting for me then, if he has seen a fire on Dragon Rock."

"I'll send one of my men to light that fire at sunset," said Brenan. "I often send a messenger into the city, and most of the fishermen live on my land. One of them will take my messenger out to the rock.

"Are you sure Haldur will see the fire?"

"He'll be looking out for it," said Nicholas. "I'm sure he'll keep watch every night."

"Then we'd all better get some sleep now," said Captain Harken. "We shall have to start as soon as it's dark."

"Supper at sunset," said Brenan, getting to his feet.

The buccaneers were taken over to another house in the courtyard. It stood near the outer wall. The door of the house opened into a large room. There was a ladder at one end of it, leading up through an open hatch into the roof.

Nicholas, Spider and the three buccaneers who were going with them were taken up the ladder, into the space beneath the roof. The floor was made of boards, and the sloping roof was just over their heads. There were two windows, one at each end. Thick sleeping bags, made of sheepskins, lay on the floor.

"Sleep first, talk later," said Spider.

Nicholas lay down by the window overlooking the wall. The others slid into sleeping bags, too, and were soon asleep.

Nicholas was tired, but he felt too excited to go to sleep at once. The sun was up now.

He gazed out over the wall, and across the heath, but he was not really looking outside. He was half-dreaming. In his imagination, he saw the city wall at midnight, and Haldur, and the rope hanging down.

Suddenly, he started. A man was moving below him, between the house and the wall. The man moved stealthily, as if he didn't want to be seen. He hadn't remembered the window.

As Nicholas watched, the man threw the end of a rope up over the wall. There was a kind of metal anchor on the end of the rope, with three iron spikes. The spikes caught between two stones, and held the rope.

The man looked over his shoulder and began to climb the rope. Nicholas recognised him. It was Mori.

Nicholas was out of his sleeping bag in a flash. He rushed over to Spider, and shook his shoulder.

"Spider!" he said. "Spider! Wake up!"

Spider had been deeply asleep, but at the first touch of Nicholas's hand, he sat up.

"What is it, Nick?" he asked.

"There's a man going over the wall. He's getting out secretly. It's Mori."

Before Nicholas had finished speaking, Spider was out of his sleeping bag and at the window. He was just in time to see Mori slip over the wall, and drop down on the other side.

"Quick! We'll tell Brenan," said Spider. "His men can move faster over the mountains than we can."

Spider and Nicholas were down the ladder and into the lower room in a minute. One of Brenan's men was sitting there by the fire.

"We have to find Brenan. Quick. It's urgent," said Spider.

The man looked up, startled.

"This way," he said, getting to his feet.

But as they followed him out of the door of the house, they saw Brenan just coming across from the great hall.

They ran over to him, to tell him what they had seen.

The moment he realised what had happened, Brenan turned, and shouted to one of his men.

"Han, Mori has left the house secretly. Get Abel and Lightfoot, and run him down. Take Garth with you. Don't kill him. Bring him back."

Han disappeared round the house. A minute later, he came back with two large, fierce-looking wolfhounds. Another man ran to join him. The drawbridge was lowered. A few moments later, they were outside, and running off across the moorland.

"They won't be long," said Brenan grimly. "Come. We'll wait in the great hall."

Spider and Nicholas followed Brenan back into the hall. Brenan stalked to a big, carved

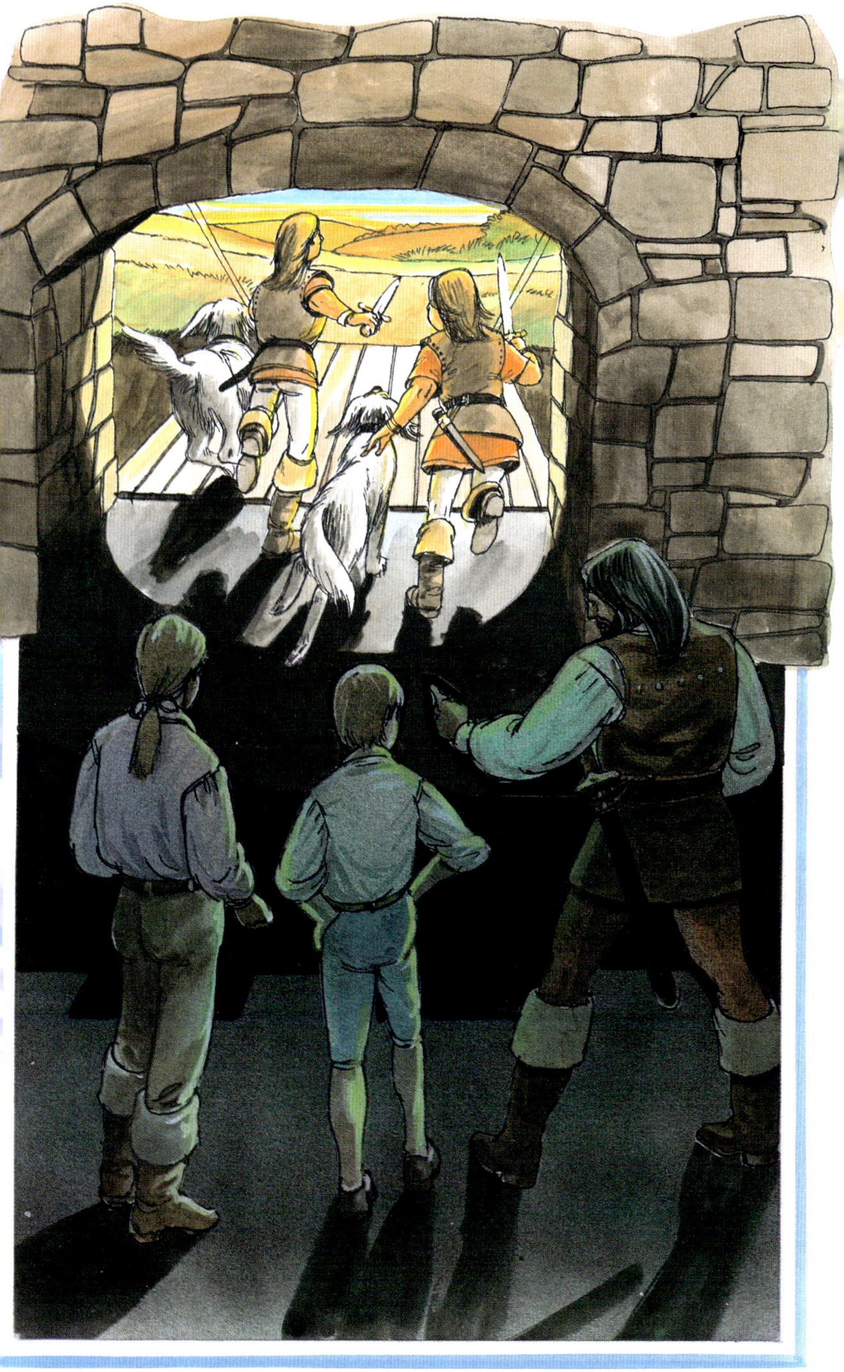

wooden chair. Spider and Nicholas each sat down.

"Tell me, boy," said Brenan. "Tell me exactly what you saw."

Nicholas told him.

"And you knew the man? You're sure it was Mori?"

"I was with him on *The Blue Whale*," said Nicholas.

"We were both with him," said Spider. "He left the ship at the end of that voyage. Martin Quinn told him to go. Mori was frightened by horned men, on The Island of the Three Hills. That wouldn't have mattered, but he ran away, and left two men on the island. So did the others, but he was the leader. They took the only boat."

"That was not the tale he told me, when he came here," said Brenan slowly.

"It wouldn't be," said Spider. "But it's the truth."

Brenan nodded. "I should have known," he said. "I wondered at the time, when he said he'd been ill, and couldn't sail east again.

"Well, here they are."

There was a growling outside, and a cry of fear. The door of the hall opened, and Mori came in, with Han and Garth on each side of him. The two wolfhounds stalked closely behind him, their noses near his heels. Mori's face was scratched, as if he had fallen in some thorns, but he wasn't hurt in any other way.

"Well, Mori?" asked Brenan. "Why did you leave this house in secret, when you knew that I had given orders for the gate to be shut?"

"I — I'd promised to meet someone," said Mori.

"Who?" barked Brenan.

"Just my son," said Mori. "No one else. He — he's a fisherman. His boat's down on the quay."

Brenan looked at him in silence for what seemed a long time.

"I don't believe you, Mori," he said at last, speaking slowly. His voice boomed out, as if it echoed in a cave. "You don't even remember your own lies. When you came here, you told me there was no one you could turn to for help. If you have a son, why didn't you go to him?"

Nicholas saw Mori turn white. His mouth opened, but didn't seem able to speak.

"You were going to Soluken, Mori, weren't you? You were serving ale this morning, with your ears wide open to everything we said."

Mori stared at him, too frightened to speak.

"Take him away," Brenan said to Han and Garth. "Lock him up, and make sure that he doesn't get away again. I'll decide what to do with him later."

Han and Garth left with Mori, with the dogs still nosing his heels.

Brenan turned to Nicholas.

"Well done, boy," he said. "I shall have something to say to my own men, for letting the man get over the wall unseen. But at least you were awake.

"Captain Harken tells me that he's adopted you as his son."

Nicholas nodded.

"He's made a good choice," said Brenan gruffly. "Go and get some sleep now, both of you. You'll need all your strength tonight. I'll see you're called at sunset."

Spider and Nicholas went back to their sleeping bags.

The other buccaneers were still in the top room, sleeping.

"I don't think I'll ever get to sleep, after all that," whispered Nicholas, as he slid into his sleeping bag.

"You will, if you give yourself a chance," said Spider. "And if you can't sleep, lie still, and rest."

Nicholas lay down, and closed his eyes. At first, he could still feel his heart thumping with excitement. But after a little while, he calmed down. Spider was right. He must get some rest. He gave a deep sigh, and fell asleep.

Chapter 6
Adventure by night

They slept all day, and were woken just before sunset.

Supper was set out on the table in the great hall. Nicholas felt too excited to eat very much. He found the waiting difficult. He always felt better, once he was doing something.

After supper, they went out into the courtyard. The other three joined them. They were all wearing dark clothes, and Spike was carrying a coil of rope. The others were tying some shorter bits of rope around their waists.

Brenan and Captain Harken came out of the great hall, and crossed the courtyard to speak to them. One of Brenan's men came with them.

"Captain Harken thinks that you will be safer, if you travel the last kilometre by boat." said Brenan. "Garth will go with you, to show you the way down the cliffs to the sea. There's a fishing boat tied up at a place we know. You can use the small boat, which lies alongside it."

Spider nodded. "That's fine," he said. "I didn't fancy walking along the quay in front of the great gates of Ramir. There'll be guards on that gate, and who knows who else may be down there? Most seamen would recognise us as buccaneers, if they saw us. And then they might start asking questions. If we slip in quietly, by boat, no one will be any the wiser."

"I hope you're right, Spider," said Captain Harken. "If you are seen, you'd better say that I thought the journey to Ikroon was too dangerous for Nicholas, and sent him back to my sister's house in the city. Tell them I sent you to look after him. It's not much of a story, but it's better than nothing."

Spider nodded. "I'll keep an eye on Nick," he said. "I only hope that he'll keep one on me!"

Captain Harken smiled. "Good luck to you all," he said. "We'll be there waiting for you, under the tower."

Brenan made a sign to the men on the towers by the gate. The drawbridge rattled down; the gates creaked open.

"A good journey and a safe return," said Brenan.

Garth led the buccaneers out through the gate and across the moorland towards the cliffs.

The night was clear, and the stars were coming out. A little wind from the sea swept over the moor. Nicholas shivered.

"Cold?" asked Spider.

Nicholas shook his head.

Spider grinned. "You'll feel better soon, Nick," he said. "You'll be all right, once we're there."

"I'll be all right," said Nicholas.

"Of course you will," said Spider.

Garth led them at a quick pace across the moor, and before long, they came to the edge of the cliffs, and looked down into the Sea Road.

They turned along the cliffs, towards the city. They hadn't gone far, when Garth turned sharply to the right, down a gully. It was the way down to the sea below.

It was a steep climb down. Garth went first, and showed them where to put their hands and feet, but Nicholas would have found it much more difficult, if Spider hadn't been there.

Spider took the rope from Spike when they came to difficult places. He dropped it down the cliff, hitching it over a rock, and holding it until Nicholas had climbed down below him, with the rope to help him.

Nicholas saw the fishing boat, as soon as they got to the sea. It was tied to a rock. A small boat swung from a rope in the stern.

A dark form rose up out of the boat, as they came to it.

"Who goes there?" asked a deep voice, speaking softly.

"The sun will set early tonight," said Garth.

Nicholas guessed that this must be a password, because the dark figure answered: "The sun will rise early tomorrow."

Then the man said, as if he were surprised: "Garth? What's afoot?"

"Nothing you need to know about, Jake," said Garth. "Brenan wishes to borrow your small boat, for his friends."

"Take it and welcome," said the fisherman. "I don't ask questions, when Brenan wants something. But you're the second man to come down the cliff today."

"The second?" asked Spider.

"Dirk went this way earlier, to light the fire on Dragon Rock," Garth said quietly. He raised his voice a little. "We'll take the boat, Jake."

Jake went to the stern of his boat, and undid the painter. He pulled the boat alongside, and tossed the painter to Garth.

Garth held the rope, saying nothing, while Spider and the others climbed into the boat as quietly as they could. (Nicholas knew that sound carries a long way, across the water.)

There was only one pair of oars. Jem took them. Spider picked up the ropes of the rudder, and the others packed themselves into the boat as well as they could. There wasn't much room.

"Good luck go with you," breathed Garth. He pushed off the boat.

Jem was a strong rower, but it was less than an hour before midnight when Nicholas, who was in the bows, saw the long stone quay ahead of them. There were fishing boats tied up along the quay, and the city wall rose up behind it.

Spider took the boat across to the far side of

the Sea Road, and made his way in, with the cliffs towering up beside them. They could see men on the quay. Some had lanterns, and moved from boat to boat. Spider watched them for a time, but he decided that they were just fishermen, visiting each other. They weren't guards. Time was passing. They must get to the quay before midnight.

They landed at the far end of the quay, where the mountains came down to the water.

The end of the quay was in dark shadow. They tied up the boat, and went swiftly across the stones to the wall.

"Now, Nicholas," Spider breathed into Nicholas's ear.

Nicholas lifted his hands to his mouth.

The call of an owl floated out into the night. The sound echoed against the cliffs.

Nicholas dropped his hands, and waited in silence. The others stood by him in the darkness.

He was just going to make the owl call again, when there was a soft plop! on the stone at the foot of the wall. It was the end of the rope.

"Up and over," whispered Spider. "There's no one watching — and the shadows are so dark here, they couldn't see us, anyway."

Jem gripped the rope, and climbed up, followed by Spike and Jory.

"Now you, Nick," breathed Spider.

Nicholas took the rope in his hands and climbed upwards. His hands banged against the wall. He felt for a foothold on the stone, and pulled himself up. Two strong hands gripped him under the armpits, and he was lifted up and through the battlements.

"Into the shadow, Nick. Across the wall," whispered Jem, putting him down.

Nicholas moved quickly across the wall to the steps, and down into the shadow below. Spike and Jory were already there, waiting. A moment later, Spider and Jem dropped down beside them. Spider had the rope in his hand.

"I can hide that," someone said in a whisper. Nicholas peered into the darkness, and saw Haldur.

"Do you want to take the rope with you?" whispered Haldur. "If you don't, I've got a hiding place for it, under a stone."

Spider handed the rope over. "We've got all the rope we need with us," he breathed. "And we may need this one here again."

Haldur took the rope, and then moved farther back into the shadows. A minute later, he was back, empty-handed.

"We can't all go through the city together," whispered Spider. "People would notice us. Jem, you find your way to the tower on your own. Spike and Jory, you go together. I'll go with the boys. We'll meet in the lane at the foot of the tower."

The buccaneers moved off softly into the darkness.

"This way, you two," whispered Spider. "We'll see Haldur safely home, Nick, and then go to the tower."

"Can't I come?" asked Haldur.

Spider shook his head. "No," he said. "We may have to fight. We shouldn't be taking Nick, but he's the only one who knows where the secret passage is. So we have to take him. But it will be safer if you go home — safer for us, as well as for you. Come on. This way."

They set off, through the dark lanes and streets of the city. Spider took them by the back ways around the big square, and back along the far side of it, to the house where Haldur lived.

Haldur climbed safely in through the open window.

"I'll be down by the wall every night for an hour at midnight, Nick, in case you need me," Haldur whispered, looking out of the window. "You won't have to light a fire. I'll go there anyway."

"It'll be dangerous after tonight, Haldur," said Spider. "They'll have guards all along the wall, if the Alarkin escapes. So be very careful."

"I'll be careful," said Haldur. "But I'll be there. You may need to come again that way."

"Yes, we may," said Spider. "All right, Haldur. But watch what you do. Don't show yourself, unless you hear the owl call. And only wait by the wall at midnight, for as long as you can count to five hundred."

"I will," whispered Haldur.

"Good lad," said Spider softly.

"Good luck," whispered Nicholas.

"Good luck go with you, too," said Haldur.

Nicholas and Spider turned away from the window, and set off for the tower.

It was after midnight, and the moon was shining down. Some of the streets and lanes were bright in the moonlight, some lay in shadow. But even where the moonlight fell, the lanes between the houses were narrow, and there were dark shadows in the doorways.

When the lane crossed other streets, they saw people walking about, but they met no one. If anyone was coming their way, Spider turned into another lane, or hid in the shadow, until they had passed.

"We'll meet them if we have to," he muttered to Nicholas under this breath. "But we won't go asking for trouble."

They had turned into a lane leading steeply up towards the tower, when they saw a man coming down towards them. He was carrying a lantern in his hand.

"Quick! This way!" Spider breathed in Nicholas's ear.

There was a flight of stone steps in the street beside them, leading up to a door in the wall above their heads. They crept swiftly up

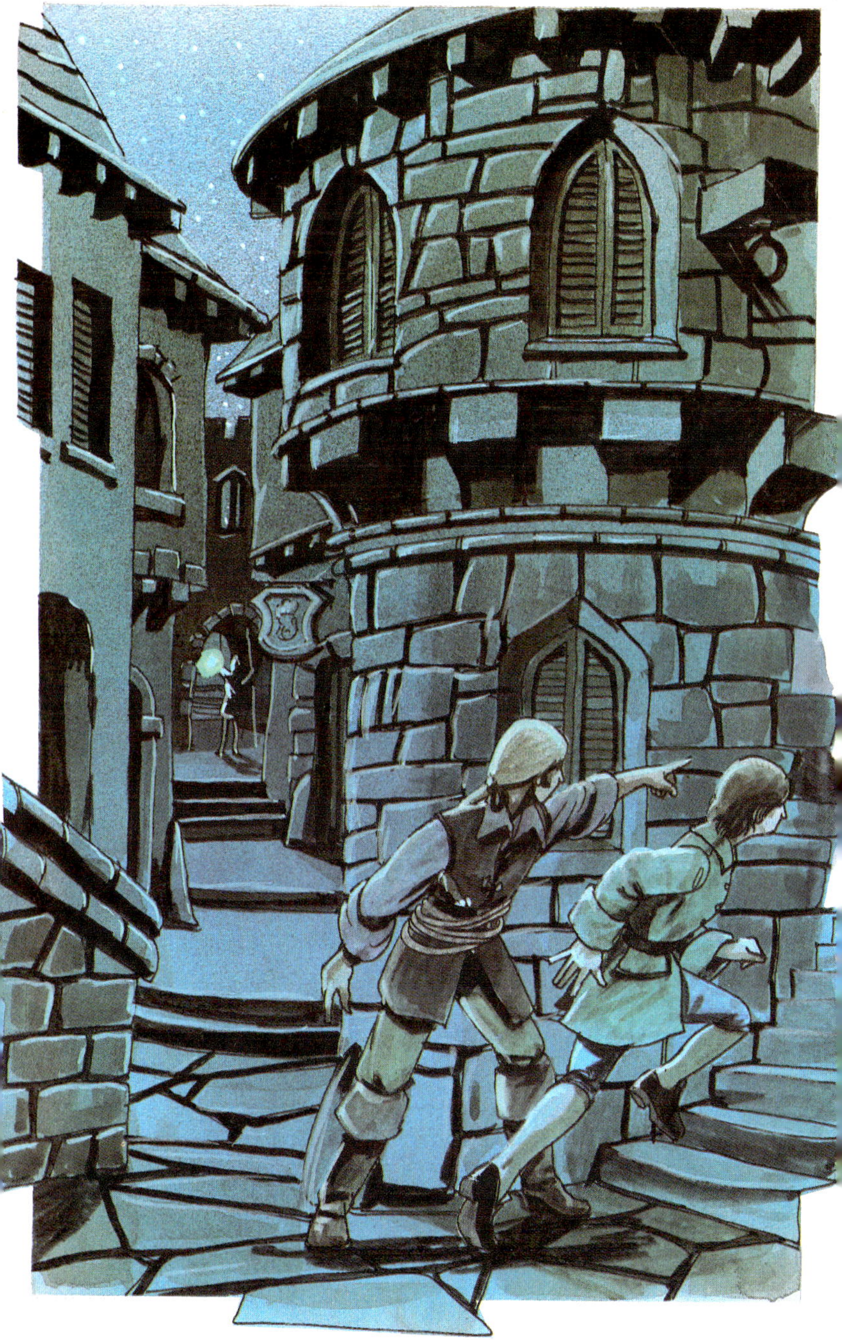

the steps, and hid behind some large pots, full of flowers, which stood on the flat square of stone at the top of the steps.

As the man came towards them, the light from the lantern touched them. Spider moved slightly, to keep in the shadow.

He touched one of the pots of flowers. It fell sideways off the top of the steps, and down into the road with a crash, just in front of the man with the lantern.

The man stopped and looked up. He lifted his lantern.

"Who's there?" he said sharply. "Come down, whoever you are, or I'll call the guard."

Before Spider could say anything, Nicholas moved down the steps into the road.

"It's only me," he said.

The man held the lantern up to his face, and looked at him.

"And who are you?" he demanded.

"I'm — I'm just a boy from one of the fishing boats," said Nicholas.

"What's your name?"

"Tobit." That was true. Nicholas's second name *was* Tobit, but he never told anyone, because people always laughed at it.

"What are you doing out at this time of night, Tobit?" demanded the man. "Stealing?"

Nicholas shook his head. "I'm not a thief," he said. "But I can't sleep indoors. I like to sleep under the stars."

To his surprise, the man laughed.

"You're like all the fisher-folk. You're still half-wild," he said. "All right, Tobit. If you would rather sleep on the cold stone, with the moon on your face, I won't stop you. But I warn you. I shall remember you. If anyone wakes tomorrow morning, and finds anything stolen, I shall know where to look."

"I'm not a thief," Nicholas protested.

The man looked at him again. "No, I don't think you are," he said. "You haven't the look of a thief, or I should take you with me.

"Well, Tobit, I'll trust you to keep honest. Goodnight, and sleep well."

He went off down the lane.

As soon as he had turned the corner, Spider dropped down into the lane beside Nicholas.

"Well done, Nick," he said. "You were lucky. And that fellow was lucky, too. I was all ready to drop a pot on his head, if he didn't believe you!"

Nicholas laughed rather shakily. His knees felt a little weak.

"Come on," said Spider. "We've only got the last bit to do now — up to the tower."

They climbed the steps at the top of the hill, and came into the lane at the side of the tower. Three shadows moved out from the wall. They were Spike, Jem and Jory.

"All right?" whispered Jory.

"So far," Spider whispered back. "Now, Nick — where's this secret passage?"

Nicholas's heart was still beating rather fast. He went up to the wall of the tower, and peered at the panel of carving, set in the stones. He put one hand in, and found the bolt. Then he pulled gently at the carving. The whole panel swung outwards in his hand.

"There you are," he whispered. "In there."

"It's a good thing Barnabas isn't here," said Spider, looking at the size of the opening. "He'd get stuck in the hole! If I'd known it was as narrow as that, Nick, I might have left Jem at home! In you go, Jory. Now Spike. Now you, Jem."

One after another, the buccaneers wriggled through the hole. There was only just room for Jem to get through, but he managed it, with a pull from Spike. Nicholas followed them.

Spider came last. "How do we shut it, Nick?" he whispered. "We can't leave it open."

"Just pull it, and push the bolt down into the stone," said Nicholas.

Spider gently pulled the end of the carving, until the panel of stone fitted back into the wall. He felt for the bolt, and shot it home.

"On we go," he whispered. "Wait! I'll lead the way. Then you, Nick. Then the others."

The other buccaneers flattened themselves

against the wall, as Spider and Nicholas squeezed by them in the narrow passage.

Their eyes were used to the dark, and there was just a little light slipping in between the holes in the carving. Spider felt his way to the stone stairs, and led the way upwards.

When they came to the room below the Alarkin's prison, Spider stopped, and looked through the holes.

"The guard's asleep," he breathed to Nicholas. "I can see him in the firelight. Who did you say he was? Gunrun?"

"Yes," whispered Nicholas.

Spider crept on. Nicholas and the others followed.

They came to the carving in the wall of the Alarkin's room. Nicholas and Spider peered in.

The fire in the room was a red glow. A figure lay curled up on the bed at one side.

"Alarkin!" Spider said softly. "Alarkin!"

The Alarkin couldn't have been asleep. He sprang out of bed, and across to the stone carving.

"Nicholas?" he asked.

"Nicholas is here," whispered Spider. "I'm Spider, and there are three buccaneers with me. We've come to rescue you, Alarkin. Listen carefully. We're going up to the roof. We'll tie up the guards, and let a rope down to your window — the one on the mountain side of the wall.

"When you see the rope, climb down it.

Captain Harken's waiting for you at the foot of the tower."

Nicholas heard the Alarkin draw in his breath sharply. "I understand," he said. "I'm ready." He went swiftly to the window.

Spider moved on, up the last steps to the turret.

"Wait here," he whispered to Nicholas.

He pushed the trapdoor back and climbed out.

In a moment, he was back again.

"You'll never believe it," he whispered. "But I think the guards are asleep. They're Soluken's men, all right! You'd never find the real guards of Ramir asleep on duty!

"Come on, Spike. You and Jory take the far guard. Jem and I will take the near one. One of you shove the gag in his mouth, while the other holds him. Whatever happens, they mustn't cry out. Untie your ropes now."

The buccaneers untied the short ropes they had fastened around their waists. They were going to use them to tie up the guards.

"You stay here, Nick! That's an order," whispered Spider.

The four buccaneers crept softly past Nicholas, and climbed down from the turret on to the roof of the tower.

As soon as they had gone, Nicholas crept out, and looked down through the little battlements on the turret.

He was just in time to see the buccaneers seize the two sleeping guards.

The guards never had a chance. Two of the buccaneers thrust gags into their mouths, and tied them behind their heads, almost before they were awake. The other two turned them over, grabbed their hands, and tied them behind their backs.

The guard caught by Spike and Jory managed to get one hand free, and started to struggle. But Spider left Jem to tie up the second guard, and helped Jory with the first.

There was very little noise. Nicholas heard one or two grunts from the guards, and that was all.

"Drunk!" said Jory in disgust, pointing to a big jug with his foot. "Drunk on duty! Soluken will never hold Ramir, with this lot!"

"Pass me the coil of rope, Jem," said Spider.

Jem turned back to the turret. Nicholas picked up the big coil of rope, which had been left by the trapdoor, and handed it to him. Then he climbed down on to the roof.

Spider took one end of the rope, and fastened it to the battlements. Then he leant over, and looked down.

He put his hands together, and hooted like an owl, just as Nicholas had done.

An answering owl call floated up from below. Captain Harken, Brenan and his men were waiting in the shadows.

Spider dropped the end of the rope down over the wall. It fell across the window below.

Nicholas peered over the battlements, and saw the Alarkin's hand grab the rope. As he watched, the Alarkin climbed through the narrow window, and slid down it.

"Now you, Nick," said Spider.

Nicholas climbed over the battlements, and gripped the rope. He slid down to the ground, fending off from the wall with his feet. Captain Harken gripped his arm, as he touched the ground. "Well done, Nick," he whispered.

The four buccaneers on the roof of the tower lowered down the drunken guards. Brenan's men took charge of them.

Then Spike came sliding down the rope, followed by Jem and Jory. Spider came last.

"Any trouble, Spider?" asked Captain Harken softly.

"No trouble at all," said Spider.

"Then we'll get away before any trouble starts," said Captain Harken. "We're ready, Brenan."

Brenan turned, and silently led the way along the wall, and back into the mountains.

Chapter 7
The escape

Nicholas didn't remember much of the walk back to Brenan's house. The Alarkin walked at the front, with Brenan and his men. Some carried the drunken guards, slung over their shoulders like two sacks of potatoes. Captain Harken and the buccaneers followed.

Nicholas stumbled along beside the others as well as he could. Once or twice, he would have fallen over a stone, but Captain Harken's hand caught him, and held him up.

"The boy's dead tired," he heard Captain Harken say to Spider.

"So he is," said Spider. "But the thing I like about Nick, is that he gets tired at the right time. When he has to keep going, he keeps going. And he has his wits about him, too! He's a good lad."

"He's more than that," said Captain Harken.

When at last they came to Brenan's house, the drawbridge was lowered, and the gates were open to welcome them.

It seemed to Nicholas as if everyone was talking at once. The fire was blazing in the great hall. There were lanterns hanging from brackets in the walls, and lighted candles on the table.

Breakfast was already set out on the table in the centre of the hall. It looked like a feast.

There were dishes of eggs, and great hams, and fish; there were plates of dark bread, brown bowls full of thick cream, and black bowls full of honey. There were piles of fruit, too.

Spider gave Nicholas a hot drink, which woke him up a little. They sat down at one end of the table. The Alarkin sat down at the other end, with Captain Harken on one side and Brenan on the other.

Nicholas was too tired to talk, but, once he started, he managed to eat a good breakfast.

As soon as they had all finished, the table was cleared and Brenan leant forward in his chair, and lifted his hand for silence.

"I must first welcome you to my house, Alarkin," he said. "No one could be more welcome. I am honoured, to have the rightful King of Ramir under my roof.

"But this is no time to make speeches. You must all rest, and I and my men will stand guard. The gates are shut, and the drawbridge is up. You will be quite safe.

"We will wake you at sunset. We will hold a meeting then, to talk over our plans.

"But now we will show you where you can sleep."

The Alarkin left the hall, with Brenan and Captain Harken. Spider, Nicholas, Jem, Spike and Jory went back to their sleeping bags in the top room of the house by the wall. The other buccaneers went off with one of Brenan's men.

Nicholas was having a hard job to keep his eyes open. He was glad to wriggle into his sleeping bag. In no time at all, he was asleep.

* * *

He was woken by the sound of a horn. It sounded loud and clear, breaking through his dreams. He sat up, and looked out of the window, over the wall.

A man was sitting on horseback by the post on the other side of the deep ditch. He held the horn to his lips, and as Nicholas watched, he blew it again.

A whole troop of men on horseback stood behind him. Nicholas couldn't see how many there were, but it looked to him like a whole company of guards. One of them, dressed in a grey cloak, trimmed with white fur, seemed to be the leader. Nicholas recognised him, and drew in his breath sharply. It was Soluken.

As the sound of the horn died away, Brenan crossed the yard below, and went into the door of the tower by the gate. A few moments later, Nicholas saw him come out on the top of the tower.

"Greetings, Soluken," Brenan boomed out, in his deep voice.

"Greetings," Soluken called back. His voice sounded high and thin.

"He won't win a shouting match, will he?" said Spider's voice in Nicholas's ear.

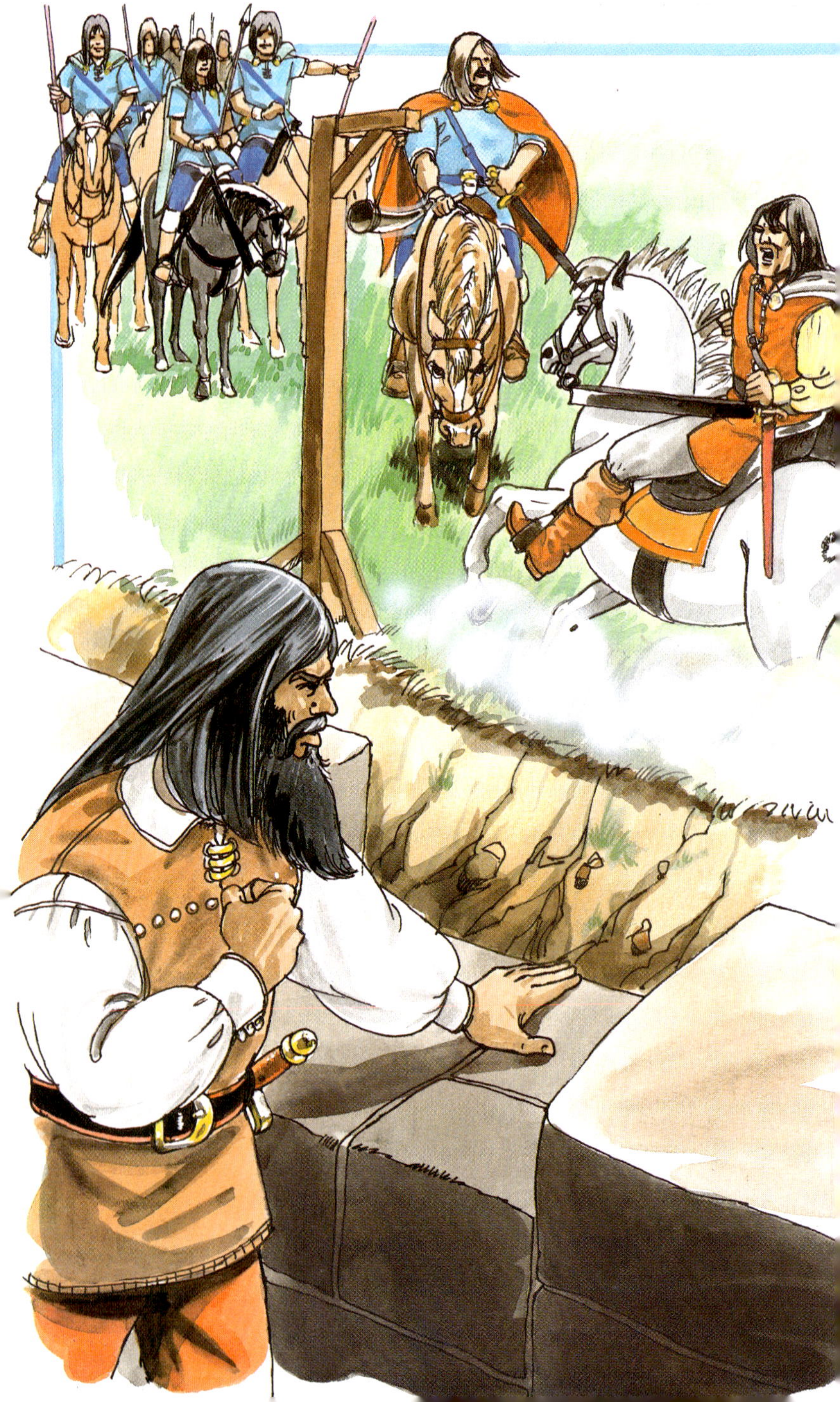

Nicholas started, and looked around. Spider was crouching just behind him, looking out of the window. The other buccaneers were still asleep.

"Hallo, Spider," said Nicholas. "What's going to happen now? Soluken's got more men than Brenan."

"Let's wait and see," said Spider. "We've got a seat in the grandstand, anyway."

"Open the gates, Brenan!" cried Soluken. "Open your gates, and let us in."

"You are welcome to come in, Soluken," said Brenan. "But it seems to me that you have rather a large number of men with you, for a friendly visit. I'm afraid that my house is scarcely big enough to hold them all."

"We are searching for the Alarkin," said Soluken. "The Alarkin wandered out on to the moors, and is lost."

"I am surprised that the Alarkin could be lost, so near the City of Ramir," said Brenan. "But I will keep a good look-out for him. His father was a good friend of mine, as you well know, Soluken. I would be glad to take care of his son, if the Alarkin should come here."

Soluken tossed back his cloak.

"The Alarkin is ill," he shouted angrily. "He is not in his right mind. If he has come to you, you must give him up."

"I did not say that he was here," said Brenan. "But if he did come here, I think that perhaps I should take care of him even better than you would, Soluken.''

Soluken lost his temper.

"Open your gates, in the name of Ramir!" he cried angrily. "Open your gates, or we will break them down!"

"I will obey the orders of the King of Ramir, Soluken. You are not king — yet," said Brenan. "And you tell me that the King of Ramir is lost."

"The Alarkin is not King of Ramir!" cried Soluken furiously. "There is a new Council. The Alarkool will be king."

"You will forgive me if I follow the orders of the Lord of Ramir, and the true Council of Ramir," said Brenan. "The Lord of Ramir said that the Alarkin should rule Ramir after him. And the rightful Council of Ramir made the Alarkin king."

"I won't argue with you any longer!" cried Soluken. "It's clear that you are a rebel. I can guess where the Alarkin is now! It will do you no good to hold out against us, Brenan. It won't help the Alarkin, either. Open your gates, in the name of Ramir, or we will break them down!"

One of the other riders, a man in a scarlet cloak, touched Soluken on the arm. He whispered something in his ear.

"I will open my gates for you, Soluken," said Brenan. "But for you alone. Send your men off a kilometre across the moor to wait for you. Then you can come in."

"Do you think I'm a fool?" cried Soluken in fury.

The rider in the scarlet cloak touched his arm again, and said something more.

Brenan stood on the tower, waiting quietly. Nicholas noticed that twenty or more of Brenan's men had gathered in the yard below, and others were quietly moving along the top of the wall, keeping well down below the battlements.

Soluken turned back towards Brenan.

"Is the Alarkin with you? Tell me that," he cried.

"I shall answer none of your questions," said Brenan. "I do not think that you come as a friend of the Alarkin."

"Then I shall set a guard on your gates until you do open them!" cried Soluken. "You'll open them soon enough, when your food supplies run low."

Brenan laughed.

"You are wise to sit and wait, Soluken, rather than fight," he cried. "Any man who tries to break down my gate is likely to get his own head broken!"

He turned, and left the top of the tower.

Nicholas saw Soluken and the man with the scarlet cloak talking together. Then the man turned to the troop of guards, and called out an order. The men rode back for fifty metres or so, dismounted, and began to make a camp. Some of them spread to the left and right.

Nicholas guessed that Brenan's house was being completely surrounded.

Finally, Soluken, with ten or eleven men, rode off in the direction of the city.

"What will happen now?" asked Nicholas.

"Let's go down and see," said Spider. "It's time we went down, anyway. It's nearly sunset."

He went over to Jem, Spike and Jory, and shook each of them awake.

"You're missing the excitement," he said, as they sat up, rubbing their eyes. "Soluken's been here, asking to come in."

He told them what had happened.

"We'd better get downstairs," said Jem. "There'll be some plan or other being talked about, by this time."

There was a jug of water and a bowl on a little table at one side. The buccaneers washed quickly. Nicholas washed too, and in a few minutes they were all on their way to the great hall.

They found the other buccaneers there already. They were sitting around the table, with Brenan, the Alarkin, and Captain Harken.

"We were going back into the city tonight," Captain Harken was saying. "I want to try to find out how many men Soluken has, and where they are stationed. And I'd like to know how the people of the city feel about Soluken and the Alarkool."

"You can't do that tonight," said Brenan.

"Not now. The best thing for you to do, Francis, is to get the Alarkin safely across to *The Silver Dolphin*.

"You should wait for the rest of the fleet, now. The city will be humming like an angry beehive, and every stranger will be questioned. When you go back into the city next time, you should have all the buccaneers in the fleet to back you up."

"Perhaps you're right," said Captain Harken. "I agree that we should take the Alarkin to *The Silver Dolphin*, if we can. That's the safest place for him just now. Soluken's men won't search the cliffs. They'll search inland. If they did see *The Silver Dolphin*, we could always put out to sea. Soluken hasn't any fighting ships."

"It's the safest place for all of you," said Brenan. "I might even let Soluken send a man in here, to make sure I'm not hiding anyone — once you've all gone!

"But I don't think I will. If Soluken leaves a company of men out there on the mountain, sitting down outside my gates, then that's one company of men you won't have to fight in the city. They'll give up soon enough, when the city is taken."

"Do you think you can hold them here?" said Captain Harken.

"I can try," said Brenan.

"You talk about us all going to *The Silver Dolphin* as if we could just walk out and go there," said the Alarkin. "Does that mean there is some secret way?"

"It does," said Brenan, with a grim smile. "When my great-great-grandfather built this house, he didn't mean to be shut up in it. The times were as dangerous then as they are now.

"There's a secret passage out into the moor. You can follow it tonight, as soon as it's dark. It will take you out beyond Soluken's men.

"The opening on to the moor isn't far beyond them. But you've a good chance of getting away, if you go after dark, and before the moon rises.

"It will be dangerous. But we'll be here, watching from the house. If they see you, we shall charge out, and try to bring you safely in."

"No," said the Alarkin quietly. "I can't agree to that, Brenan. There are four times the number of men you have, out there on the moor.

"I don't like leaving you at all, with a company of Soluken's guards camped outside your gate. But if we can find the fleet, we can return with the buccaneers, after we have taken the city. So we'll go by your secret passage. But if Soluken's men see us, we'll have to run for it — or do our own fighting. You must stay here, inside your walls. You'll only be killed or captured, if you come outside them."

"I can't agree to that," said Brenan.

"You'll have to," said the Alarkin. "It is an order. I shall not go, unless I have your promise to stay inside the walls."

Brenan took a deep breath, and opened his mouth as if to reply. The Alarkin looked straight at him. His head was thrown back, and for the first time, Nicholas thought that he looked like a king.

Brenan stared into his eyes for a moment. Then he nodded his head.

"Very well," he said. "You have my promise. I am a faithful subject of the King of Ramir."

"Then I will go," said the Alarkin. "You will come with me, Captain Harken, and Nicholas, and all the buccaneers. They mustn't be found here, if Soluken's men do break in."

"We're ready to leave whenever you choose," said Captain Harken.

"It's not dark enough yet," said Brenan. "And you may as well have supper before you go. You may have a long night ahead of you."

"Very well," said the Alarkin. "We'll leave as soon as it is dark."

Nicholas thought that one of the things he would always remember about Brenan's house would be the meals. In no time at all, the long table in the great hall was laden with food, and they all had supper.

By the time it was over, the sun had set,

and it was beginning to get dark. They waited until an hour before moonrise. Then Brenan led the Alarkin and the buccaneers down into one of the cellars in the house by the wall.

Brenan carried a lantern, and so did Spider, who walked in the middle of the group, and Jem, who came last.

The cellar was used for keeping wine. It was full of barrels, and it was lined with great stones.

Brenan took them over to one of the walls. He moved a barrel out of the way, and then lifted a stone on the floor at his feet. He put his hand into a hole below the stone, and pulled something.

Then he pressed against two of the biggest stones in the wall.

The stones swung sideways. There was a narrow passageway behind them.

"I'll take you to the far end, and close the way behind you," said Brenan. "I promised to stay within the walls of my house — but this is part of the house, too."

"You will return here, when you have shown us the way," said the Alarkin.

Brenan nodded. He stepped into the passageway. He seemed to fill it with his great body, but he moved along it easily, as if he knew the way.

The others followed him. Nicholas kept near Spider.

The passage was lined with stone, like the cellar, and it smelt damp.

They walked on, in single file, for what seemed to Nicholas a long time. Then Brenan stopped. The men behind him stopped, too.

The message came back from the front, whispered over his shoulder by each man: "Put out the lanterns."

Spider blew out his lantern, and a few moments later, the passage was in darkness. Nicholas felt his heart beginning to beat faster.

Spider moved forward a little. As his eyes got used to the darkness, Nicholas saw a faint light ahead. They moved slowly onwards, towards it.

Then Nicholas felt the air on his face, and saw Spider climbing through an opening over his head. He felt forward, and his hands touched a ladder. He climbed up the ladder, and out of a hole on to the moor.

"Down! Keep down!" Brenan's deep voice breathed in his ear.

Nicholas crawled forwards, and looked around.

They were in the middle of a patch of bushes. Brenan was kneeling by the opening, and the others were crouching down.

Nicholas crawled after Spider, and crept in under a bush. The other buccaneers climbed, one by one, out of the secret passage to join them.

"This way!" whispered Captain Harken. "Keep your heads down below the bushes. Goodbye, Brenan. Good luck go with you.

We'll drive Soluken's men away from your house before long."

The buccaneers moved off in single file in the darkness, leaving Brenan to shut the entrance to the passage, and go back to the house.

The buccaneers crept to the edge of the big patch of bushes, which hid the exit from the secret passage. Nicholas and Spider were at the front now, just behind Captain Harken and the Alarkin.

When they came to the open moor, there was a pause.

"Brenan said there was a deep ditch here," Nicholas heard Captain Harken say softly, "Can you see it?"

"Not yet," said the Alarkin. He looked back. "Spider, move over to the right, and see if you can find the ditch," he whispered. "Nicholas, you go to the left."

Nicholas moved carefully along the edge of the bushes to the left. He kept low down, so that there was no chance of his being seen.

He hadn't gone very far, when he saw a long patch of darkness on the heath. He looked closely, and saw that it was the ditch. He turned, and crept quietly back to the others.

"It's this way," he whispered.

The Alarkin followed him, as he led the way back to the ditch. The buccaneers climbed down into it one by one. They could stand up, now. Their heads were below the level of the ground. They set off at a quick walk.

The ditch ended a kilometre farther on, towards the edge of the cliffs. It grew shallower and shallower, and at last they found themselves walking on level ground again. But there was no need to crouch down any more. Higher ground lay between them and Brenan's house. No one from there could see them now.

Captain Harken led the way along a sheep track westwards towards the sea. Nicholas glanced up at the sky. The moon was just rising, and the stars were out. He felt a little wind from the sea blowing on his face.

They came to the top of the cliffs. They had been walking for about an hour, when Nicholas heard Spider say sharply: "Who's that?"

His hand came down on Nicholas's shoulder, pressing him down to the ground. The buccaneers scattered to left and right off the path, and lay down, hiding among the heather on the moor.

Nicholas raised his head a little, and looked out between the stems of the plants. He saw no one at all for a few minutes. And then a man came into view, a long way off, coming along the path towards them. Nicholas thought that Spider must have very good eyes, to have seen someone in the dark, so far away.

The man came nearer and nearer. Nicholas felt his heart beating. Was it one of Soluken's men? They could capture him, of course. There seemed to be only one. But perhaps there were others behind him.

Then he heard Spider say: "It's Tom Gold!"

"So it is," said Captain Harken. "Keep down, the rest of you, for a minute."

He got to his feet. The man walking towards them stopped, and Nicholas saw his hand go to his belt.

"Tom!" called Captain Harken softly. "Tom Gold!"

"Captain Harken!" Tom Gold cried in surprise. "I was coming to you with a message. I didn't see you, in the dark."

"We're all here, Tom," said Captain Harken. "The Alarkin, too. What's the message?"

"*The Blue Whale*'s back," said Tom Gold. "The fleet had been delayed by the storms, and *The Blue Whale* found them more quickly than we expected. The fighting ships of Ramir will anchor outside Hidden Harbour before morning."

Chapter 8
White owls calling

The buccaneers gathered round Tom Gold, slapping him on the back in delight. The ships of Ramir were sailing back to the city! Nicholas felt for a moment that it was all over, that the city was theirs again. He felt as if he were walking on air, and he knew that the other buccaneers felt as he did.

It was the Alarkin and Captain Harken who brought them back to earth.

"We still have to take the city." The Alarkin's voice broke in on the cheerful talk. "And we want to take it with as little fighting as possible. The ships of Ramir will soon be back. But the buccaneers can't just sail up to the city and demand to be let in. Soluken's men would close the gates, and man the walls."

"I think we should decide some things at once," said Captain Harken. "We haven't much time, if we want to get into the city in secret. It won't be long before some shepherd on the hills sees the fleet. The news will soon travel to Ramir. Can we hold a council here, Alarkin?"

"Of course," said the Alarkin.

They found a bare patch of ground among some rocks, and sat down in a ring.

"Now, Captain Harken," said the Alarkin. "Tell us what you have in mind."

"It will take us all day to reach the city from here, going across the moor, but we could do it by midnight," said Captain Harken thoughtfully. "We shall be still farther away, if we go back to the ship."

"But we must go back to the ship," said the Alarkin. "We must meet the buccaneers, and sail with them back to the city."

"You should go to meet them, Alarkin," said Captain Harken. "But not the rest of us. I have been thinking how we can take the city, and I have a plan. I wish I knew how many men Soluken has, but I don't think we've time to find out now.

"My plan is this: I will go towards the city with the buccaneers who are here now. We'll make our way down to Jake, the fisherman. Jake's the man who lent Spider the small boat last time. He's one of Brenan's men.

"Brenan told me before we left, that Jake would still be anchored by the cliff. We could get there before sunrise, and hide on board until it's dark. Then we'll sail to the quay in the fishing boat. We'll signal to Haldur, and go over the wall at midnight.

"In the meantime, Alarkin, you must go back to *The Silver Dolphin* with Tom Gold. You won't meet any of Soluken's men now. We're too far from Brenan's house.

"You didn't see anyone as you came along, Tom?"

"No one at all," said Tom Gold.

"Good," said Captain Harken. "Then we

shan't be needed to guard you any longer, Alarkin.

"As soon as the fleet arrives, you must take command, and sail for Ramir. There is still a chance that you will get there before anyone knows you're coming. If the fleet is as near as Tom says, you should be able to reach the quay outside the city just after midnight tomorrow night. The wind is from the south. The ships will be able to sail right up the Sea Road.

"The buccaneers must anchor the ships, and row ashore in the long boats, to the great gate in the city wall, which opens on to the quay.

"By that time, we should be hiding in the city, near the gate. As soon as we see the ships, we shall attack the men who are guarding the gate. They won't be expecting us. There shouldn't be more than nine or ten of them, and we shall have all the advantage of surprise.

"All we shall try to do, is to open the great gate — and let the buccaneers pour into the city.

"I don't think Soluken's men will make much of a fight of it, once they know that the city is full of buccaneers.

"But everything depends on surprise. If Soluken once knows that the fleet is on the way, his men will be ready. The gates will be shut, and Soluken's men will be guarding the walls. So we must act now, and be ready to enter the city tomorrow night.''

''Suppose something happens, and your plan goes wrong,'' said the Alarkin. ''Suppose you're seen climbing the wall? Or suppose the gate is too well guarded? What happens then?''

''Then the buccaneers will have to fight their way into the city,'' said Captain Harken. ''I know we shall have to be lucky, to take the city by surprise. But we have a chance to do it.''

''If we're seen, or if someone stops us, there will be a fight — but without us there would be a battle for the city anyway. We've nothing to lose, by trying to capture Soluken's men before they are ready for us.

''And if we are lucky — well, then we shall save a lot of lives. I think we should go.''

''I wish I could go with you,'' said the Alarkin.

''I wish you could,'' said Captain Harken. ''But you will be needed with the fleet. You must be there to take command — to tell the High Captain what has happened, and to bring the fleet back to Ramir.''

The Alarkin thought for a moment.

''Very well,'' he said. ''We'll start at once.''

They all got to their feet.

''You'll take the Alarkin to *The Silver Dolphin*, Tom,'' said Captain Harken to Tom Gold. ''Tell Martin Quinn what our plans are. *The Blue Whale* and *The Silver Dolphin* should sail out of Hidden Harbour now, to meet the ships as they come north.''

''Aye, aye, Captain,'' said Tom Gold.

''Good luck go with you, Alarkin.''

''And with you.''

The Alarkin and Tom Gold set off along the path towards Hidden Harbour.

''Now we must turn north,'' said Captain Harken. ''I'd like to get down to Jake's ship in the Sea Road before dawn, if we can. You went that way only last night, Spider. You know where the fishing boat is. You take the lead.''

They started back along the path at the top of the cliffs. Spider led the way, and they travelled quickly. They all knew how important it was to get there before daylight.

Nicholas followed Spider with the rest. He was beginning to feel tired, but he wasn't going to let anyone know that. He breathed in deep breaths of the cool night air.

They came to the way down the cliffs just as dawn was breaking.

They clambered down towards the sea. Nicholas found that he was able to climb down this time without help. One or two of the buccaneers needed a hand in places, but Nicholas managed on his own. He was getting better at climbing.

''I should be getting better, too,'' he thought to himself. ''I've been getting a lot of practice.''

The fishing boat was anchored in by the cliffs, just where it had been before. As Nicholas climbed down on to the last rocks by the water, he looked up and saw Jake, sitting on the deck, watching them.

"The sun will set early tonight," said Spider.

Jake got slowly to his feet, and moved across to the side of the boat. "The sun will rise early tomorrow," he said. "What do you need this time?"

"Brenan sent us to you again," said Spider. "Can you take us in to the city?"

"The small boat is still tied up to the quay," said Jake. "But you're too many for that, anyway. How did you get back, last time?"

"We went back across the mountain to Brenan's house," said Spike.

Jake nodded. "I thought you might have done," he said. "I'll take you, of course, if Brenan says so. I can get the small boat at the same time."

"Have you anyone else on board now?" asked Captain Harken.

"Just my two sons," said Jake. "We sail this boat together."

"We can't sail until tonight," said Captain Harken. "Can we hide on board your boat until it's dark?"

Jake stared at him. "Captain Harken, isn't it?" he said slowly.

"Yes," said Captain Harken. "But I don't

want anyone to know I'm here. Brenan said that you could be trusted to say nothing, Jake. Can your sons be trusted, too?"

"We're all Brenan's men," said Jake. "But I'd do what you asked me, Captain Harken, even if you didn't come from Brenan. And so would my sons. It's an honour to have you on the boat.

"Come on board, all of you. You can hide here till nightfall."

As they climbed on board the fishing boat, Jake opened the door into the little cabin, in the middle of the ship.

"Wake up and come out," he said, speaking to someone inside. "We've got visitors."

Two young men came out of the door, rubbing their eyes.

"Move aside, and let the visitors in," said Jake. "They don't want strangers to see them. And if anyone asks you, you haven't seen them yourselves."

The two men moved into the bows, without a word. They stood there, staring at the buccaneers.

"The cabin's yours," said Jake.

"Thank you," said Captain Harken. He went in, and the others followed.

There was only just room for all the buccaneers inside. There was a table in the middle, with two bunks on either side of it.

"You'll want food," said Jake, standing in the doorway. "Sit down, and we'll bring you some."

He stepped back, and made a sign to his sons. Nicholas was glad of the fresh air blowing in through the open doorway. Everything in the boat smelt of fish.

"We'll take it in turns to get some sleep," said Captain Harken. "We'll have to stay inside, now it's daylight. There may be other fishing boats in the Sea Road."

Nicholas looked out, and saw that Jake's sons were lighting a fire on the rocks.

Before long, Jake handed in a great dish of fried fishcakes. The buccaneers were hungry, and the fishcakes were soon eaten.

When they had finished, they shut the cabin door, and settled down to rest. There was very little room, but Nicholas managed to curl up in a corner of one of the bunks, and go to sleep.

He was woken by a shout from outside the ship.

"Ahoy there! What ship are you?"

"*The Scarlet Fish* — a fishing boat, out of Ramir," he heard Jake call back.

Nicholas sat up. All the buccaneers were awake, listening. Nicholas saw that some of them had pulled their pistols out of their belts.

"Have you seen a young stranger on the cliffs, or on the sea?"

"There's been no stranger here," called Jake.

"There's a young prisoner escaped from the city," shouted the first voice. "Soluken's ordered everyone to keep an eye open for him. He's offered ten pieces of gold, to any man who brings him in.''

"That's a lot of money," said Jake slowly. "Who is this prisoner?"

"That's no business of yours or mine," shouted the first voice. "But if you see him, take him in."

"He'll not come this way," said Jake. "I've never been a lucky man, when there was a chance to earn some gold."

"Well, you may be, this time. Keep your eyes open!"

The ship sailed past them, and was gone.

The buccaneers pushed their pistols back into their belts.

"You don't think Jake will guess that we know anything about that prisoner, do you?" whispered Jem.

"Of course he will," said Spider. "Jake's slow, but he's no fool. He knows that Nick and I took his small boat to the city the other night. He'll guess what we were doing there."

"Are you sure we can trust him?" whispered Jory. "Ten pieces of gold is a lot of money for any man. It's a small fortune, for a fisherman."

The cabin door opened, and Jake looked in.

"That one has gone," he said. "But there may be others. You'll have to stay inside all day. Is there anything you need?"

"We're all right, Jake," said Captain Harken. "We'll keep our heads down."

"I'll bring supper in at sunset," said Jake.

He shut the door.

"I'm sure that we can trust Jake," said Captain Harken quietly. "We have to, anyway. But he's one of Brenan's men. He won't let Soluken buy him, with ten pieces of gold. I'm sure of that. Let's rest while we can."

They settled down to rest, the men talking quietly.

Nicholas went back to sleep.

* * *

He woke at sunset, when the door of the cabin opened, and Jake came in with a plate of fried fish.

"The wind's still from the south," he said, as he put the dish down. "It will be an easy sail down the Sea Road to the City of Ramir."

"We should be there before midnight," said Captain Harken.

"Then we'll sail as soon as it's dark," said Jake.

Captain Harken waited until Jake had shut the door behind him. Then he said quietly: "With this wind, the fleet will be able to sail down the Sea Road, up to the very gate of the city."

"You said that we should have to be lucky,

Cap'n," said Spider. "Well, our luck's holding out, so far. Mind you, I've always been lucky, when I've had young Nick with me!"

The others laughed, and began to eat the fried fish.

Slowly, the light faded, and it grew dark outside.

After a time, they heard Jake and his sons pull in the anchor, and set the sails.

The door opened, and Jake looked in.

"Time to go," he said. "Do any of you want to come outside, as we sail in? No one could recognise you now. It's too dark."

"We'll keep hidden, Jake," said Captain Harken. "If anyone saw the boat with extra men on board, he might wonder who you had with you. And we don't want anyone asking questions."

"The boy could come out," said Jake. "I often have my youngest son with me, and he's not here tonight. There's not much room in there."

"All right, Nick," said Captain Harken with a nod.

Nicholas squeezed out of the cabin. Jake shut the door again, and Nicholas drew in deep breath of fresh air.

"You'd best get up in the bows," said Jake. "You can help us keep a bit of a watch. Sing out, if you see anyone on the shore. We shall have our eyes on the water."

Nicholas climbed forward into the bows of

the little ship, and stared out into the dark. The great cliffs on each side of the Sea Road rose up like high, black walls. The stars were out. He could see the moonlight catching the top of the mountains on the west side of the Sea Road, but down between the great cliffs, the water was still dark.

The wind was from the south, but it was very light, and they sailed slowly.

Nicholas looked up at the cliffs. A little spark of light was bobbing along the cliff edge, on the eastern side.

"There's someone up there," he called softly, pointing towards it.

"Looking for you, I expect," said Jake. "It's a good thing we left when we did."

They sailed on, into the darkness.

Before long, Nicholas saw the lights of the City of Ramir ahead. The city was built on a slope, from the mountains down to the sea. Great lanterns were always lit at the gates of the city at night, and he could see lights in the windows of the tallest buildings, which were higher than the city wall.

Jake took the fishing boat over towards the quay, where Spider had rowed the small boat, only two nights ago.

A bigger boat was moored close to the cliff, two or three hundred metres out from the quay. There was a lantern burning on the stern, and as they passed, a voice called out: "Who goes there?"

"Jake, the fisherman, and his boat *The Scarlet Fish*," Jake called across the water.

"What are you doing, sailing in at this time of night? The gates have been shut since sunset."

"I'll tie up by the quay," said Jake. "We've had a good catch. I want to be at the fish market first thing in the morning."

"You should have been in before this."

"The fishing was too good. We found a school of fish late in the evening," called Jake.

"You'd better go in, and tie up for the night at the quay."

"What's wrong, then?" shouted Jake.

There was no answer. Nicholas saw a man standing by the lantern, watching them as they glided past, but the man asked no more questions.

Nicholas thought to himself that Jake spoke slowly, but he was quick to think of the right answers.

One of Jake's sons moved into the bows. As the fishing boat reached the quay, he jumped ashore with the end of a rope, and tied her up to an iron ring.

Nicholas looked down the quay, and saw two men coming along it. They were both carrying lanterns, and Nicholas could see that they had pistols in their belts. He knew that they must be Soluken's guards.

"What ship is this?" one of them asked.

"*The Scarlet Fish*," said Jake.

"What are you doing here?"

"Bringing in a load of fish for the market tomorrow."

"We'll come on board," one of the guards called.

He was moving towards them, when the other said: "What's the use of getting yourself covered in fish scales? Do you want to see the inside of every miserable little boat that ties up at the quay?"

The other guard hesitated. He looked down into the boat. Jake and one of his sons stood there quietly, staring back at him. Nicholas saw the other son, who was still on the quay, move slowly across, till he was behind the two guards.

"Who's on board?" asked the first guard.

"Me and my two sons, and the ship's boy," said Jake.

"Oh, leave them," said the second guard. "They're only fishermen. We'll be changing watch at midnight. It's nearly midnight now. They'll be waiting for us in the guard house."

They turned away, and walked back down the quay.

No one on the fishing boat moved, until the men with the lanterns had reached the great gate. A small door in one of the low towers beside it opened, and they disappeared inside.

Jake opened the door into the cabin.

"All clear, Captain," he said softly.

"That's twice they've challenged us. They must be keeping a special watch tonight. But you've time to get across the quay, before the next guards come down this way."

Captain Harken and the other buccaneers came swiftly out of the cabin and climbed ashore.

"Can you wait here, Jake?" whispered Captain Harken.

"I'll have to," said Jake. "I'm waiting till the fish market opens."

Captain Harken laughed softly. "So you are," he said. "Then we'll see you later. Thank you for your help."

"You've only to ask me any time, Captain, and I'll do all I can," said Jake softly.

Captain Harken moved across the quay into the deep shadow under the wall, and the others followed him.

They moved along to the point where the wall turned inland, and the cliff came down to the sea. Captain Harken made a sign to Spider.

"Let's hear that owl call, Nick," Spider whispered in Nicholas's ear.

Nicholas put his hands up to his mouth, and blew into them.

The first call sounded a little shaky, as if the owl were short of breath. But the second call echoed clearly against the mountain side.

A moment later, it was answered by another owl call, from the other side of the city wall.

Nicholas felt the excitement mounting inside him. Haldur was there!

The rope dropped down from the wall. A moment later, and Spider was climbing up and over the battlements. Quickly and quietly, the others followed. Nicholas scrambled up after Jem. Captain Harken came last.

"Down off the wall, into the shadow," whispered Captain Harken.

The buccaneers moved swiftly down the steps into the dark courtyard. Captain Harken took a last look back, down the Sea Road, the way they had come. Then he, too, climbed quickly down the steps. Haldur stopped for a moment to untie the rope, and followed him.

"Well done, Haldur," whispered Captain Harken. He turned to the others. "The ships should be here soon. I saw no sign of them, as we sailed in, but they must be here before long. They'll sail in without lights. The buccaneers may be anchored now, and rowing the long boats in towards the quay.

"We'd better hide in the shadows for a time, and then creep over to the gates. We mustn't move too soon. Spider, can you creep back on to the wall, and keep watch? Make the owl call, if you see or hear a sign of the buccaneers. That boat out there may challenge them. Soluken's men are keeping a sharp watch tonight."

Spider crept back up the steps. The others waited in the darkness of the courtyard. The windows of the houses were shuttered, and there were deep shadows.

They seemed to have been standing in the courtyard for a long time, when Spider scrambled softly down the steps.

"I think I saw a movement out to sea," he breathed in Captain Harken's ear. "But we'll have to move, anyway. There are guards coming along the top of the wall."

Captain Harken moved across the courtyard, and softly opened the wooden gate.

"This way," he breathed.

The buccaneers flitted across the courtyard like shadows, under the archway and into the lane.

They were not a moment too soon. Captain Harken had only just time to close the gate, when two of Soluken's guards came walking along the top of the wall, carrying lanterns.

They had just reached the top of the steps leading down into the courtyard, when the buccaneers heard a sound out at sea. Voices carry a long way over the water at night. They couldn't hear what was said, but it sounded like a challenge.

Then a horn sounded, echoing across the water.

"This way," whispered Captain Harken. "We must take the gate. Quickly. The buccaneers are coming."

They ran swiftly along the lane to their left,

keeping to the shadows as much as they could.

The lane ran along the inner side of the wall. They saw it opening out ahead of them, and realised that they were coming to the main gates.

Captain Harken stopped. "We'll walk right up to the gate and jump the guard," he whispered. "The guards will be in the towers, watching the sea. Spider, you take five men, and take over the tower on the other side of the gate. The rest of us will take the tower on this side."

They moved quickly forward, and came out of the shadows.

A guard was standing at the foot of each tower, facing towards the city. Each guard had a pike in his hand.

Captain Harken and the buccaneers strode suddenly out of the shadows and up to the gates.

The guards lowered the pikes in front of them, to bar the way.

"Who are you, and what do you want?" cried one of them. "Don't you know that you can't leave the city at night?"

But before Captain Harken could reply, the second guard recognised him.

"Buccaneers!" he cried. "Treachery! Sound the alarm! The buccaneers are here!"

Jem and Jory leapt on him, knocking his pike sideways. Captain Harken drew his cutlass, and slashed the other pike, as the first guard turned on him.

Ten or eleven other guards, hearing the shouts, came running out of the towers on each side of the gate. In another moment, the space before the gates was full of fighting men.

In the first few minutes, Nicholas got a blow on the head that sent him spinning into a corner. He dropped to the ground in the shadow, and for a time he knew nothing more.

When he came to himself, the fight was still raging. More guards had come down from the walls. They were driving the buccaneers back down the lane. Nicholas staggered to his feet. He heard shouts from the far end of the lane, and saw more of Soluken's men, with lanterns in their hands, blocking the way. They were all fighting with cutlasses. No one could fire a pistol, for fear of hitting one of his own side.

There was a shout from the quay on the other side of the wall.

"Open the gates! Open the gates, in the name of the King of Ramir!"

None of the guards heard it. They were fighting too fiercely, and shouting to each other.

Nicholas looked about him. He was feeling dazed, and a little sick. He suddenly realised that there was no one guarding the gate. All the guards were driving the buccaneers back

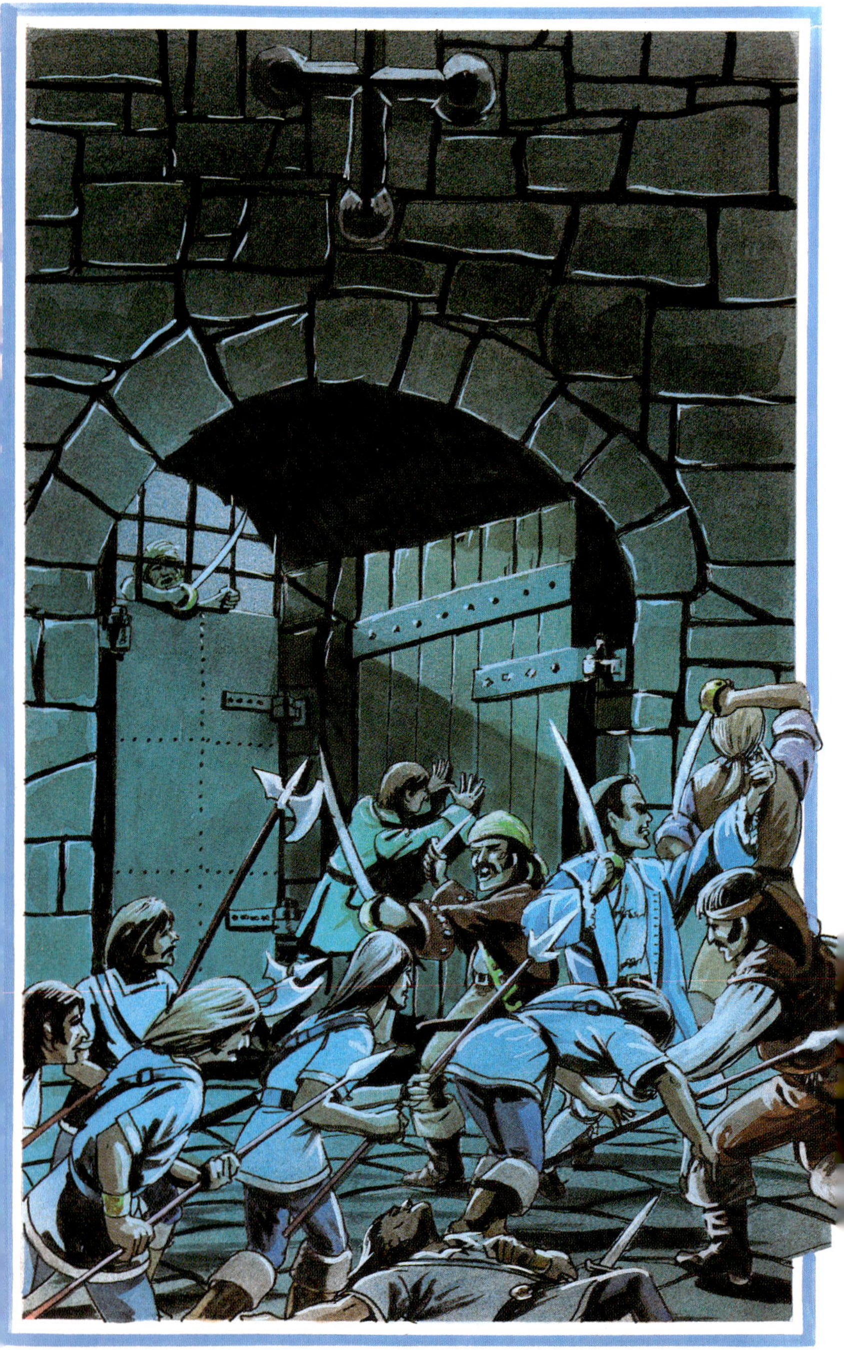

down the lane. Nicholas staggered over to the great wooden doors. They were held shut by two great heavy bolts of wood. He got his shoulder under them. With a big heave, he lifted first one end then the other, and let them fall to the ground.

He dragged the wooden doors open. There were still two big gates, shut fast, between him and the buccaneers.

The buccaneers saw him through the gates. They let out a great shout. The buccaneers close to the gates seized them in their hands, and tried to break through. But the gates were made of iron. They held fast.

The noise was terrific. The buccaneers were shouting and banging at the gates, drowning the sound of fighting in the streets. Nicholas was deafened by the noise. He still felt dazed by the blow on his head.

Then he saw Barnabas Brandy. Barnabas was among the buccaneers closest to the gate. He was shouting something, but Nicholas couldn't hear what he said. Barnabas was pointing to one of the towers by the gates.

Nicholas gazed at him, without understanding what he meant. Then, suddenly, he knew. There must be something in the tower, which would open the gates.

Nicholas turned, and stumbled into the tower. He found himself in a little square room. There were stairs up one side of it. But on the other side, there was a big round wheel, like the wheel of a ship. It stood out from the floor.

Nicholas grabbed the wheel, and turned it.

There was a great cheer from the buccaneers outside. The gates were beginning to move. He turned the wheel faster and faster, until it would turn no longer. Then he moved back to the door of the tower, to see what was happening.

The street outside was full of men. The buccaneers were pouring into the city through the open gates.

There were so many buccaneers in the street, that he couldn't get out of the tower. The crush of men was too great. He turned, and went up the stone stairs on the far side of the room.

There was another room above, and more steps leading upwards. Nicholas went up the steps. He came to an open trapdoor, leading to the top of the tower. He climbed thankfully up, and went out into the cool night air.

The moon was high in the sky now, shining down on the Sea Road. The sea in front of the quay was full of small boats, and more boatloads of buccaneers were rowing in towards the city, and leaping ashore. Out on the water, beyond the boats, he saw the fighting ships of Ramir. They were anchored there, side by side, line upon line of them. The Sea Road was full of them. The ships of Ramir had come home, to fight for the Alarkin, their new king.

Chapter 9
Soluken

Nicholas leant on the wall between the battlements, taking in great breaths of the cool night air. His head ached, and he still felt dazed. But as he stared at the ships, his head began to clear, and he forgot his own feelings. The fighting ships had come back in time! That was all that mattered now. The buccaneers would take over the city, and the Alarkin would be crowned King of Ramir.

Nicholas wondered where the Alarkin was. He turned, and moved to the other side of the tower. He looked out, into the city.

The narrow lane, which ran along the inside of the city walls, was to his right. He could see another lane on the other side of the great gates, to his left, running along the inside of the wall. Below him, the buccaneers were still coming in, but there were fewer of them now. The main rush was over.

In front of him, a wide street ran up towards the great square, in the middle of the city. There was no one in that street. Most of the fighting seemed to be along the walls, and in the narrow lanes.

Suddenly, Nicholas stiffened. A long way up the wide street, a man came into view. He stood there for a moment, and then turned, and ran towards the square. He was too far away for Nicholas to see who he was. But, before he was hidden by the houses, Nicholas saw that the man was wearing a grey cloak, trimmed with white fur.

No one else had seen him. The buccaneers were all in the lanes, or on the wall.

Nicholas glanced back at the harbour. The last buccaneers had come ashore. A few men were standing guard over the empty boats, which were tied up along the quay. But that was all. He must find someone, and tell them about the man in the grey cloak. Soluken mustn't escape.

As he turned towards the steps, to go down into the street, he heard someone calling his name.

"Nicholas! Nicholas, are you there?"

Nicholas ran down the steps inside the tower. The Alarkin, a cutlass in his hand, was standing in the doorway.

"There you are, Nick!" cried the Alarkin. "I was afraid Soluken's men might have hurt you. The battle's over. The city is ours.

"The buccaneers are taking prisoners, and rounding up any stray guards who have escaped in the lanes. But it really is all over.

"I came back to find you. Barnabas said that it was you who opened the gates."

"Did you catch Soluken?" cried Nicholas.

"Soluken? No," said the Alarkin. "You haven't seen him?"

"I think so," said Nicholas. "I saw a figure in a grey cloak, with white fur on it. He was at the top of the street that leads to the great square."

"Come on," said the Alarkin.

The Alarkin ran up the wide street, and Nicholas ran after him, panting. They reached the great square.

"Let's try the Council Chamber," said the Alarkin. "The record books will be there — the lists of Soluken's men, and a record of what Soluken has been doing since he became regent. He'll want to burn those, now. Come on."

He ran across the square towards the great stone house, where the Council Chamber was, with Nicholas at his side.

They pushed open the door and ran up the wide stone staircase, two steps at a time.

As they came to the passage outside the room where the Council of Ramir always met, they saw a grey cloak whisk around the far corner.

"There he is!" cried the Alarkin, dashing along the passage. "This way!"

They turned the corner, and saw a flight of stone steps, leading upwards.

The Alarkin rushed up the steps, with his cutlass still in his right hand. Nicholas kept just behind him.

They came into another room, but it was empty. There were more stairs on the far side, leading up to an open door, which led out on to the roof of the building.

"He'll not escape now," panted the Alarkin. He was across the room in a moment, racing up the steps.

Nicholas followed. His side was aching, and he was almost out of breath, but he struggled up the steps as quickly as he could.

The door led straight out into the open air. The Alarkin, with Nicholas behind him, rushed out on to the flat roof of the building — and stopped.

The moon was shining down, and it was almost as light as day. But they saw no one. The Alarkin, cutlass in hand, gazed around him.

"Drop your cutlass!" A cold voice sounded behind them.

They spun round, and found themselves facing Soluken. His grey cloak was thrown back. He was holding two pistols, one in each hand.

"Drop your cutlass, Alarkin!" he commanded. "If you don't, I shall shoot the boy first, and then you."

The Alarkin hesistated a moment. Then, as Soluken cocked one of his pistols, the Alarkin dropped his hand, and let his cutlass fall to the ground.

"Move to one side, boy," said Soluken, looking at Nicholas and jerking his head to the left.

There was no help for it. Nicholas moved across a little way to one side.

"Farther!" said Soluken angrily. "Be quick, and don't try any tricks, or I shall shoot the Alarkin."

Nicholas moved farther across.

"Get the cutlass, Gunrun," commanded Soluken.

The opening to the stairs was protected from the weather by a little stone hut, with the doorway leading directly on to the roof.

Soluken must have been hiding behind it. As Nicholas stood there, getting his breath back, Gunrun moved out from behind the hut into the moonlight. He went over to the Alarkin, and picked up the cutlass.

"Tie his hands behind him," said Soluken.

The Alarkin suddenly sprang sideways, and stood clear of Gunrun.

"I'll not be your prisoner again, Soluken!" he cried. "You'll have to kill me. And if you do that, you know what will happen to you. You can't get away. Your guards are prisoners, and the city is full of buccaneers. You dare not kill me, if you value your own life!"

"I shall lose nothing by killing you!" said Soluken between his teeth. "Do you think the buccaneers will let me go, even if I let you live? Do you think they will put me in prison? Of course they won't. They'll hang me. I'm not a fool.

"No, I've nothing to lose, Alarkin. If you don't come with me, as my prisoner, I've no hope of getting out of this city."

"And I will never go with you, Soluken," said the Alarkin, tossing back his hair.

"Then, if I have to die, I'll take you with me!" cried Soluken.

He lifted his pistol.

"Stop!" Someone had come out of the door on to the roof, and stood there in the moonlight. Nicholas stared at him. It was the Alarkool.

"You go too far, Soluken," said the Alarkool. His voice was clear and cold, but he was breathing hard, as if he had been running. "The Alarkin is my brother — the son of the Lord of Ramir. How dare you threaten his life!"

Soluken swung his left arm sideways. His second pistol, which had been aimed at Nicholas, was now pointing at the Alarkool.

"So!" he said. "Both the sons of the Lord of Ramir are against me! You're fools, both of you! Neither of you could rule without me. You are nothing, without me! Do you think you can stop me now, Alarkool? Why do you think I have been helping you? If we had won, who would have been the real Lord of Ramir?"

He laughed, and his laughter was so wild that Nicholas wondered if he had gone mad.

"I've lost," he cried, "but at least if I have to die I'll take both the sons of the Lord of Ramir with me!"

He cocked the pistol in his left hand, and aimed it at the Alarkool's head.

From the moment that the Alarkool had arrived on the roof, Nicholas had been

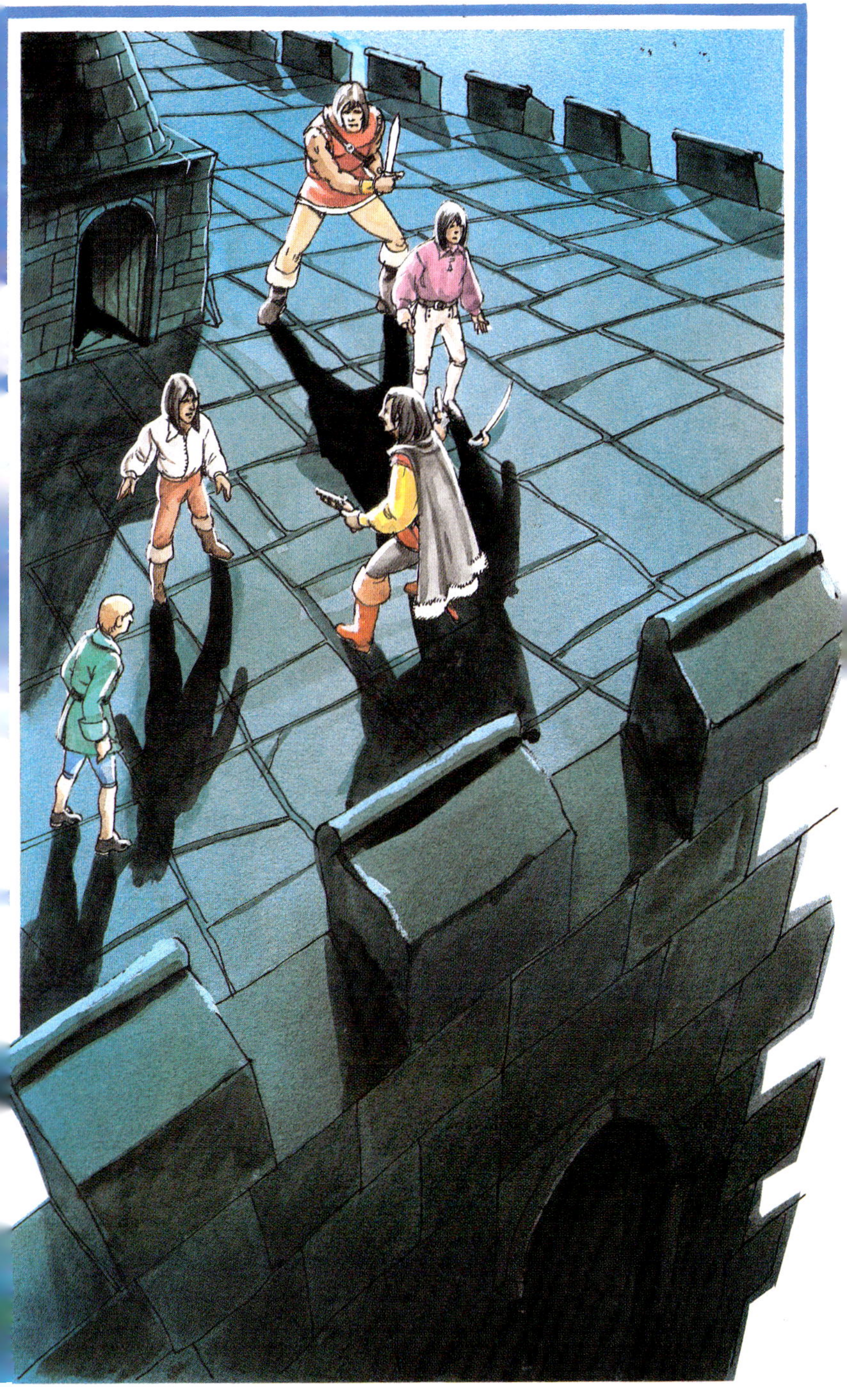

moving slowly forward. Soluken, whose eyes were only on the Alarkool and the Alarkin, had not noticed him.

As Soluken pulled the trigger, Nicholas leapt forward as if he were making a rugby tackle. The pistol went off, as Nicholas caught Soluken's knees, bringing him to the ground.

The Alarkool dropped to the roof. The Alarkin sprang forward, but before he could reach Soluken, Gunrun had leapt across, and seized the regent in his great arms.

"Traitor!" he cried, lifting him up into the air, and holding him over his head. "Traitor! You have killed the Alarkool! You have killed the greatest man who ever lived in Ramir!"

Before the Alarkin could stop him, Gunrun rushed to the side of the roof, and hurled Soluken down into the square below.

* * *

Nicholas slowly picked himself up off the stones of the roof. The Alarkin was already kneeling beside the Alarkool. The Alarkool looked very white, and his eyes were closed.

Gunrun looked down into the square. Then he moved quickly across to them, and dropped beside the Alarkool. Nicholas heard him sobbing.

The Alarkool opened his eyes.

"He got me in the shoulder," he said faintly. He saw Gunrun. "Never fear,

Gunrun," he said. "I'm not dead yet. The Council of Ramir will still have a chance to hang me."

His head dropped sideways.

"He's fainted," said the Alarkin. "Have we anything to stop the bleeding?"

Without a word, Nicholas pulled off his shirt, tore it into strips, and handed them to the Alarkin.

The Alarkin pulled out his knife, and cut the Alarkool's clothes away from the wound. With Nicholas's help, he began to bandage it up.

"Gunrun," said the Alarkin. "Go down into the town, and find Captain Harken, or one of the other captains from the fleet. Tell them what has happened. Tell them to send a surgeon as quickly as they can. We shall need a stretcher."

"Is he dead?" Gunrun whispered.

"No, no. He's just fainted," said the Alarkin. "I don't think the bone is broken. Nicholas knocked Soluken sideways, and spoilt his aim. But he'll need a surgeon. Be as quick as you can, Gunrun."

"You — you'll not let them hang him, will you?" asked Gunrun.

"The Alarkool shall live. You have my promise, Gunrun. And I won't let them keep him in prison — or you, either. Go and get help, as fast as you can."

Without another word, Gunrun got to his feet, and stumbled off down the stone stairs.

The Alarkin, with Nicholas's help, finished bandaging his brother's shoulder. They laid him gently back on the stone tiles.

"That's the second time you've saved the Alarkool's life, Nick," the Alarkin said, sitting back on the stones. "He may not seem very grateful, but he doesn't forget."

"Do you think he'll live?" asked Nicholas.

"I'm sure he will," said the Alarkin. "The surgeon will get the bullet out, and clean up the wound. And he saved my life, that time. The Council of Ramir will remember that, and so shall I.

"Well, Nick, you opened the city gates, and you saved the lives of both the sons of the Lord of Ramir. Soluken would have shot me, after he'd shot the Alarkool. How do you feel?"

"I feel a bit sick," said Nicholas.

The Alarkin laughed. "I wouldn't be without you for anything, Nick!" he said. "You always say something I don't expect! You'll be going back to that other world of yours before long, I'm afraid, but you must come back to Ramir as soon as you can. And stay with us for as long as you can. There will always be a place for you, here in Ramir."

Footsteps sounded on the stairs. Captain Harken, followed by Gunrun, Barnabas Brandy, and four buccaneers came racing up the steps and out on to the roof.

"You're here more quickly than I thought possible," said the Alarkin.

"Gunrun met us in the square," said Captain Harken. "We were just coming to look for Soluken."

"Did you find him?" asked the Alarkin.

Captain Harken nodded. "He's quite dead," he said. "They will bury him outside the walls tonight. He was a traitor to the end."

"A traitor to my brother, as well as to me," said the Alarkin. "I'll tell you the story later. But now my brother needs a surgeon."

"Three of the ships' surgeons are turning some of the rooms below into a hospital," said Captain Harken. "The Alarkool is not the only man who has been hurt. But it looks as if Soluken is the only man who has been killed. When they saw that the buccaneers were inside the city, Soluken's men laid down their arms."

"I'm glad of it," said the Alarkin. "Have they been made prisoners?"

"Yes," said Captain Harken. "One or two may have escaped over the mountains, but not many."

One of the buccaneers had brought a stretcher with him. They lifted the Alarkool on to the stretcher. Now they carried him through the door, and down the staircase.

The Alarkin looked at the sky.

"It will soon be dawn," he said.

"Yes," said Captain Harken. "And it really is the dawn of a new day, this time. A day on which you will be the only rightful

King of Ramir. There'll be no more regents now, Alarkin. You will be king and ruler."

The Alarkin stared out over the city.

"It seems strange," he said.

"You'll get used to it," said Barnabas Brandy cheerfully. "Kings always do.

"Well, Nick. You're still alive?"

"He's very much alive," said the Alarkin. "But I'm not sure that I would be, if he hadn't been there."

"Both of you look only half alive," said Captain Harken. "It's been a long night. We must go down to the king's rooms. The cooks are bringing food there. We can hear the story then."

"Come, then," said the Alarkin.

He turned, and led the way down the steps, towards the Council Chamber.

Chapter 10
The rightful King of Ramir

For the next three days, Nicholas spent most of his time with Haldur, and Haldur was one of the happiest boys in Ramir. On that strange morning when the Alarkin became the rightful King of Ramir, Captain Harken took Nicholas across the square to his sister's house. He was given a bed in Haldur's room, fresh clothes, and, best of all, a bath.

When he had rested, and had some food, Haldur took him out into the city. Everywhere, people were standing about in the streets and in the squares, talking together.

The story of how the buccaneers had taken over the city became more and more exciting, as everyone told new parts of the story to everyone else. There were even people who said that the buccaneers had a young magician with them, who had touched the city gates, and the gates had flown open by magic! There were some very strange glances at Nicholas as he went by.

Nicholas tried not to notice them. He remembered how hard it had been to shift the great wooden bars, and his search for the wheel to open the gates. Haldur listened to everything, and laughed with delight.

Wherever Nicholas went, buccaneers came up to him to talk, and make friends. They clapped him on the back, and told him how well he had done.

Some of the buccaneers took the boys on board one of the great ships in the Sea Road. They met men who had sailed in the Ocean of Ramir all their days. And everywhere, Nicholas found friends. He was glad that people didn't ask him where he came from. Everyone knew that he was Captain Harken's adopted son, and the Alarkin's friend. That was enough for them.

It was one of the happiest times in Nicholas's own life. He spent all day in the city with Haldur, and at night Captain Harken came to his sister's house to sleep. Nicholas would have been even happier, if he had not felt that the time was coming when he would have to go back to his own world. It was a strange feeling, but every time he saw the moon, it seemed to him that a silver ring was beginning to take shape around it.

He tried to warn Haldur that he might have to go soon, but Haldur didn't want to think about it.

On the evening of the third day, the Alarkin sent for Nicholas. Spider brought the message, and took him across the square, back to the great house where the Council Chamber was.

They went up the stairs, past the door of the Council Chamber, to the rooms where the Lord of Ramir had once lived, and where the Alarkin lived now.

There were two guards standing outside the door, leading to the Alarkin's rooms, but when they saw Spider and Nicholas, they stepped back, and opened the door for them. Nicholas and Spider went inside.

The Alarkin, Captain Harken, and three of the Councillors of Ramir were sitting by the fire.

"Come and sit down, Nicholas," said the Alarkin, pointing to an empty chair.

Nicholas went over to the fire and sat down. Spider took up his stand behind the Alarkin's chair. Nicholas could see that Spider was now the Alarkin's own special guard and messenger.

"There was a meeting of the Council today, Nicholas," said the Alarkin, "the true Council of Ramir, not the one Soluken made.

"And the true Council of Ramir has named me again as the rightful King of Ramir, as they had done before. But this time, there is to be no regent. So I am now the ruler of Ramir.

"In a month's time, I shall be crowned. I would have liked you to be there. I wanted to have you beside me, when the crown, which you gave me, was at last set on my head.

"But Captain Harken tells me that he thinks you may not be with us then, so I have sent for you now, to thank you for all you have done."

He looked at Captain Harken.

"It's the moonlight, Nicholas," said Captain Harken. "I've noticed that the moonlight always seems somehow to grow brighter, as the time comes for you to go — and for a night or two before you come back to us. I often know when you're coming, these days. It's growing brighter now, even though the moon is no longer full.

"I don't want you to leave us, boy. You know how glad we are to have you with us. But the moonlight is changing, and I didn't want you to go back without knowing what is happening in Ramir."

Nicholas swallowed.

"I know," he said. "I've noticed the moonlight myself, this last night or two. It's almost as if I can see a great silver ring growing around the moon."

Captain Harken nodded. "You'll be back again before long, Nicholas," he said. "And there'll always be a welcome for you in Ramir. But I guessed that you might be going to your own world for a time. There is a place for you in that world, too. There must be. If you can't see that place now, you will one day. You're the kind of person who makes a place for himself, in any world. And you'll find friends there, too."

"Captain Harken's right, Nicholas," said the Alarkin. "But you must come back to us whenever you can."

Nicholas remembered the man who had moved in next door to the house where he lived in the city. This time, he would see Andrew Tregarth and his son, Alan, when he went back through the ring.

"I think perhaps I shall find friends there now," he said. "But I'll never forget Ramir. I'll always come back."

He thought for a moment. "What is going to happen to the Alarkool?" he asked. "You promised him his life. I remember that. Is he getting better from his wound?"

The Alarkin smiled. "Yes, he is," he said. "The bullet from the pistol struck his shoulder, but the bone wasn't broken. He is recovering well.

"The Council have agreed to leave his punishment to me, because, in the end, he saved my life.

"I have talked to him. He doesn't want to stay in Ramir, now that I am king. I think that perhaps he is right. He will do us no harm. He has promised that, and the Alarkool will keep his word. But he needs to be his own master.

"I shall give him one of the fighting ships of Ramir. It's being made ready for him now. He will explore the ocean. Perhaps he will find a country where he wants to live. Perhaps he will spend his life exploring, and come home to Ramir in the end. That is for him to decide. I have said that he must go away from Ramir for seven years. But after that, he can come back, if he wants to.

"Some of Soluken's men are going with him, to man the ship. There were good men among them, and he has chosen the best of them."

"What will happen to Gunrun?" asked Nicholas.

"He is going with the Alarkool," said the Alarkin.

"And what happened to Brenan? Did Soluken's men attack his house?"

"No. They were still camped around the walls, when they heard that the fighting ships were in the Sea Road. They came back to Ramir, and surrendered."

"I'm glad the Alarkool is going free," said Nicholas. "And I'm glad Gunrun's going with him. Gunrun doesn't care about anyone, except the Alarkool."

"I'm glad, too," said the Alarkin. "I don't want men to be shut up in prison. Nor do you."

Nicholas gave a great sigh. "It's the end of the adventure," he said.

The Alarkin laughed. "It's the end of one adventure, Nicholas," he said. "But the end of one adventure is the beginning of another! That's the way things have always happened in Ramir."

They sat round the fire, talking, until the early hours of the morning. Food was brought to them, and they had a supper that was like a feast.

Then, at last, the Alarkin got up to go.

"Goodnight, Nicholas," he said, smiling. "I hope I shall see you in the morning. But if I don't, I shall see you again before long. Good luck go with you!"

Captain Harken and Nicholas left the room. They went down the stairs, and out into the great square.

The moonlight seemed even brighter than before.

They were halfway across the square, when Nicholas felt Captain Harken's hand on his shoulder.

"It's coming, Nicholas," said Captain Harken. "I can see the silver ring. Good luck go with you, boy. Come back to us soon. I shall be watching for you!"

Nicholas drew in his breath. He looked up at the sky. A great ring of silver light was swirling above the square. As he gazed at it, it dropped lower and lower, until the light was all around him.

For a moment, he saw Captain Harken, through a kind of silver mist. Captain Harken was smiling, and he lifted his hand.

Nicholas lifted his own hand in reply. Then the silver light around him changed to white fire. The flames were cold, and did him no harm. But when they died away, he found himself standing in front of the picture of the silver ring, back in his own world.